Praise for *Return to Uluru*

"Mark McKenna's fascinating and infuriating narrative of frontier injustice delivers a heady blend of true crime mystery, masterful historical research, and an eloquent call for reconciliation and social justice. With a story as resonant in North America as in McKenna's Australian homeland, *Return to Uluru* convincingly outs the 'heroes' of frontier expansion for what they truly were: architects of atrocities who quite literally were allowed to get away with murder, so long as their victims were Indigenous peoples, their culture, and their way of life."

—Edward Humes, Pulitzer Prize–winning journalist and author of *The Forever Witness*

"Mark McKenna sets the highest standard for truth-telling of the kind that Australians so urgently need if they are to live in this country with honor. I feel sure that this book will become an Australian classic, not the first of its kind, but certainly the most powerful narrative I have read of frontier injustice and its resonance in our lives today." —Marcia Langton, author of *Welcome to Country*

"Mark McKenna has exposed the wounded heart of Australia. Never has a history of our country so assumed the power of sacred myth. *Return to Uluru* is a spellbinding story of death and resurrection."

—James Boyce, author of *Born Bad*

"In illuminating one incident at Uluru in the 1930s, Mark McKenna casts a larger light on the culture and ideology of that era—harsh and brutal in so many ways, yet also uncomfortably recognizable."

—Robyn Davidson, author of *Tracks*

RETURN
TO
ULURU

RETURN
TO
ULURU

The Hidden History of a Murder
in Outback Australia

MARK McKENNA

DUTTON

DUTTON

An imprint of Penguin Random House LLC
penguinrandomhouse.com

LIBRARY OF CONGRESS CATALOGING-IN-PUBLICATION DATA

Names: McKenna, Mark, 1959- author.
Title: Return to Uluru / Mark McKenna.
Description: New York : Dutton, Penguin Random House LLC, [2022] | Includes index.
Identifiers: LCCN 2022017138 (print) | LCCN 2022017139 (ebook) |
ISBN 9780593185773 (hardcover) | ISBN 9780593185780 (ebook)
Subjects: LCSH: Aboriginal Australians—Australia—Uluru/Ayers Rock (N.T.) |
Aboriginal Australians—Australia—Uluru/Ayers Rock (N.T.)—Death. |
Police shootings—Australia—Uluru/Ayers Rock (N.T.)—History—20th century. |
Aboriginal Australians, Treatment of. | Aboriginal Australians—Social conditions. |
Aboriginal Australians—History. | Uluru/Ayers Rock (N.T.)—History—20th century. |
Uluru/Ayers Rock (N.T.)—History. | Australia—Race relations.
Classification: LCC DU398.A9 M35 2022 (print) | LCC DU398.A9 (ebook) |
DDC 305.899/15094291—dc23/eng/20220420
LC record available at https://lccn.loc.gov/2022017138
LC ebook record available at https://lccn.loc.gov/2022017139

Printed in the United States of America
1st Printing

Book design by Nancy Resnick

For Edwin Ride

CONTENTS

CONTENTS

RETURN
TO
ULURU

THE STORY OF
KUNIYA AND LIRU

The Kuniya (python) woman came from far away in the east to hatch her children at Uluru. She carried her eggs strung around her neck like a necklace and brought them to rest at Kuniya Piti on Uluru's northeast corner. There she left the eggs on the ground.

Kuniya camped at Taputji and hunted in the nearby sandhills. As she left and entered her camp, she formed deep grooves in the rock. These grooves are still there.

One day, Kuniya had to draw on all her physical and magical powers to avenge the death of her young nephew, also a Kuniya. He had enraged a group of Liru, or poisonous brown snakes, who traveled from the southwest to take revenge on him.

They saw him resting at the base of Uluru and rushed upon him, hurling their spears. Many spears hit the rock face with such force that they pierced it, leaving a series of round holes that are still obvious. The poor Kuniya, outnumbered, dodged what he could but eventually fell dead.

When news of the young python's death reached his aunt on the other side of Uluru, she was overcome with grief and anger. She raced along the curves of the rock to Mutitjulu Waterhole, where she confronted one of the Liru warriors, who mocked her grief and rage.

Kuniya began a dance of immense power and magic. As she moved toward the Liru warrior, she scooped up sand and rubbed it over her body. Her rage was so great that it spread like a poison, saturating the area at that time.

In a fearsome dance she took up her *wana*, or digging stick, and struck the head of the Liru. But her anger was now beyond restraint, and she hit him again across the head.

He fell dead, dropping his shield near Mutitjulu Waterhole, where Kuniya herself remains as a sinuous black line on the eastern wall. The blows she struck are two deep cracks on the western wall, and the Liru's shield, now a large boulder, lies where it fell.

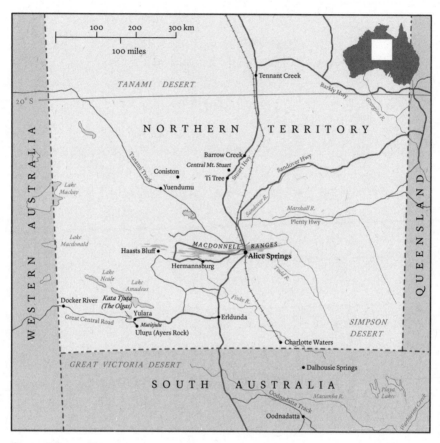

Central Australia

PART ONE

THE DEAD HEART?

A traveller may now describe Central Australia as a heart-breaking wilderness.

J. W. Gregory, *The Dead Heart of Australia*, 1906

Marree, South Australia, 2013

1

YOKUNUNNA

In November 2019, I visited the South Australian Museum in Adelaide to see if a certain man's skull was among the collection of human remains held in the museum's Keeping Place. A number of archival collections had been checked and a forensic anthropologist was attempting to match the man's skull with the unprovenanced remains thought most likely to belong to him. He had been murdered in 1934. But the forensic anthropologist could only positively identify the skull.

Museum officials Anna Russo and Professor John Carty and I decided that we would travel together to Uluru (formerly known as Ayers Rock), a huge iconic monolith more or less in the center of Australia that is home to the Aboriginal people, the Anangu. There, we would inform Sammy Wilson, chair of three community organizations—Mutitjulu Community Aboriginal Corporation, Uluru–Kata Tjuta Board of Management, and the Central Land Council—that the Indigenous person whose skull this was had been identified. He was in fact the granduncle of Sammy Wilson. His name was Yokununna.

Before we headed for Uluru, Anna and I drove to the large

factorylike building in a nearby Adelaide suburb where the museum houses the human remains in its collection. Years of chasing down the events surrounding Yokununna's killing at Uluru in central Australia had led me to this nondescript repository of horrors. We entered a vast space with little natural light and walked through several rooms, signing in as we moved from one area to the next. When we reached the room where Yokununna's skull was stored, I noticed a number of wooden boxes stacked in the corner, draped in the Aboriginal flag.

The provenance of these human remains had been established, and now they were waiting to be collected by elders and returned to Country. Nearby, medium-size cardboard boxes containing Aboriginal remains that were moved from the University of Adelaide in 2017 were stored on four shelves.

Yokununna's skull rested in Box 39. Anna took the box from the shelf and laid it on the table; she turned on an overhead lamp, put on white cotton gloves, carefully removed the skull, and placed it on tissue-like paper. With the stark white light bearing down from above, the words etched in capitals on the crown were clearly visible: YOCKANUNNA [sic] COMPLETE SKELETON. As Anna explained, this naming was unusual. Perhaps the skull was so labeled because Yokununna's remains were crucial evidence in the 1935 Commonwealth Board of Inquiry into Yokununna's death.

We noticed the missing initiation tooth and the crazing on the skull's surface: a thin, spidery web that indicated it had spent considerable time in the ground before exhumation. The slight yellowing of the bone was probably caused by tissue residue or the chemicals that may have been used to clean the skull. Eighty-five years after Yokununna's death, his remains were still subject to the invaders' gaze; still the captive object of inquiry and examination. Anna placed the skull back in the box and we washed our hands before walking into the next room.

There, stacked on shelves from floor to ceiling, were more unprovenanced remains that had come to the museum from Adelaide University—mandibles, hip bones, collarbones, vertebrae, and countless others—filed in numbered cardboard boxes. Perhaps Yokununna's postcranial remains were here, but testing the contents of every box would be an expensive and prolonged process. It was also possible that Professor John Cleland, who headed the board of inquiry into Yokununna's death, or someone else could have handed them over to the university's medical school for teaching purposes, in which case they would have been discarded long ago.

Above me, on the very top shelf, standing upright and wrapped tightly in plastic, were casts made of the heads of Aboriginal men and women by the archaeologist and ethnologist Norman Tindale from the 1930s. The thickness of the plastic that encased them made it impossible to discern any features.

This grotesque mausoleum—evidence of the racism and violence committed by the state against Australia's Indigenous people over so many years—existed in a permanent limbo. With their origins unknown, the human remains cannot be returned to Country. Yet they cried out for a Keeping Place that would pay them due cultural respect. As for Tindale's scientific monuments to inhumanity, the subjects' communities will guide journeys back to Country and make sure these traces of their ancestors' spirits return home safely. They cannot be destroyed—that would erase the truth. Nor can they be placed in public view, for that would only perpetuate the injustice. We drove back to the museum, discussing the next steps in the long journey back to the families at Uluru.

Seen for so long as barely human, Aboriginal people had suffered the same fate as stuffed animals exhibited in the Adelaide museum. They were shot, collected, studied, objectified, and categorized, a people and their cultures marked as primitive curiosities, destined to be dispossessed by their usurpers. Yokununna's remains were one among thousands.

Aboriginal remains were collected by the South Australian Museum from the late nineteenth century, but the practice began from the moment the British arrived in Australia in 1788. Private and state institutions throughout Australia and overseas hold vast collections of human remains and ethnographic material, which, in the name of scientific racism and an allegedly superior British civilization, were either traded, raided from resting places and burial sites, souvenired during the frontier wars, or stolen from Aboriginal people across the continent. By the early twentieth century, the South Australian government declared that "all native remains found on Crown lands" were to be brought to the museum in Adelaide, a policy that continued until the 1960s. Today, the museum board "cares for almost 5,000 ancestral remains, both Australian Aboriginal and from overseas nations." Of the 4,500 Aboriginal ancestors, about 3,700 are from South Australian burial sites. Since the late 1980s, the museum has worked with Aboriginal communities to repatriate remains and the Tindale casts.

Australian white supremacist culture bears responsibility for this history. But there was one white man who played a leading role in it.

Inspector Bill McKinnon in the Jubilee Day Parade, Alice Springs, 1951

2

"MORE OR LESS LONELY AND FRIENDLY PEOPLE"

Bill McKinnon was already accustomed to an itinerant life when he arrived in Stuart, then the administrative capital of the Commonwealth territory of Central Australia, on Saturday, June 6, 1931. On the train from Adelaide, he gazed out the window, thinking how barren the landscape looked. Alighting at the railway station in "drizzling rain," he encountered a tiny frontier outpost built from stone and galvanized iron with a population of little more than two hundred people. On the platform to welcome him was Constable Robert Hamilton, a First World War veteran, who, to McKinnon's surprise, hailed from Nambour, his hometown in southeast Queensland. McKinnon was barely thirty—lean, brash, and tough—a no-nonsense raconteur with a sharp tongue and unyielding determination. He'd arrived as the most recent recruit to a police force of nine men working for the Public Service of Central Australia, a region created with the stroke of a legislator's pen in 1926. After years of drought and the onset of the Depression, it would remain a separate Commonwealth territory for merely another week, before it was subsumed into the Northern Territory. Two years later, in August 1933—four years after the railway arrived and transformed the movement of livestock and people to and from central Australia—Stuart would be renamed Alice Springs. The new man had arrived and he intended to take charge. Bill McKinnon had found his place in the world. He would spend the remainder of his working life as a member of the Northern Territory Police Force.

In contrast, the first three decades of McKinnon's life were testament to the mobility of many Australians in the early twentieth century. He was born on June 16, 1902, in a timber shack on his father's "selection" at North Creek, Ballina, in northern New South Wales (NSW). His great-grandparents, who had emigrated from the Isle of Skye and the Scottish Highlands, were married on the banks of the Shoalhaven River by the Reverend Samuel Marsden. His family moved to Queensland when his father, lured by cane growing and dairying, decided there was greater opportunity farther north. As the youngest child, McKinnon always believed he was his mother's favorite. In September 1922, when he sailed for Sydney from Brisbane, his family saw him off: "I have never forgotten," he recalled years later, "the emotional feelings during those long moments while the ship was moving away from the wharf and starting downstream. My mother was heartbroken."

In Sydney, he found work as a wireless operator before taking a job in the engine room of RMS *Niagara* and sailing as far afield as Vancouver. In 1923, a few weeks after his twenty-first birthday, he joined the NSW Mounted Police, only to take off back to Queensland with "itchy feet" little more than eighteen months later. Over the next four years, he sailed the world on trading ships (once as a tally clerk with a "nice chap" by the name of Errol Flynn) and worked as a warder in St. Helena and Brisbane jails. He detested his role at St. Helena—"a nasty, morale destroying job"—where he was "under strict discipline" from those above him and administered "the same strict discipline to the inmates" under his control. Violence and self-harm were part of daily life in the prison. On one occasion, he "saw

McKinnon on Bondi Beach, 1920s

a man in a cell hanging from a strip of blanket tied to a bar . . . cut him down with a blunt knife and revived him." The confined nature of the work—"one spent the whole of [one's] working hours behind stone walls or locked in a tower on the walls"—drove him to despair.

After eighteen months he resigned and accepted a new position as "Warrant Officer 2nd Class in the Rabaul Town Police," on the island of New Britain, 375 miles east of New Guinea. Following a brief period of German rule from the late nineteenth century until the First World War, when it fell to Australian forces, Rabaul had become part of Australia's "Mandated Territory of New Guinea" in 1921. In December 1927, McKinnon sailed into Rabaul Harbor. It was only twelve months after an infamous punitive expedition led by Australian forces and New Guinea "native" police. Eager to avenge the killing of four Australian men at Nakanai in the center of the island, they allegedly used a machine gun and bombs to kill at least eighteen people. Although the policy of driving Aboriginal people from their lands onto reserves in Australia differed from practices in New Guinea, where the village remained the center of colonial administration, the violent methods used to instill fear and obedience in the native population were strikingly similar. McKinnon joined other Australian police, many of whom had fought in the First World War and, like himself, had served in state police forces at home. For a while, he was appointed "acting jailer," supervising a racially segregated prison that consisted of Chinese convicted for gambling or smoking opium, a small number of Europeans, and more than 150 "natives" imprisoned behind "a high barbed wire fence." Each day, he took the "physically fit prisoners" to the jail quarry, where they picked and knapped stone, occasionally marching native "murderers"— "handcuffed and secured together"—to the nearby wharf, where they boarded a ship that took them back to their village. Once there, they were immediately hanged in full view of their community.

Off duty in Rabaul, he discovered an enduring love of photography, inspecting the surrounding country "with camera and walking stick," led by his "native" guides. When forty-four sperm whales were washed up onto Matupi Beach on September 13, 1928, a day after a severe tremor, he "sent snapshots of the scene to the *Brisbane Courier*," where they were quickly published. It would be the first of many missions of self-assigned photojournalism completed with his self-timer and tripod. When he climbed volcanic craters near Rabaul, he made sure to photograph himself surveying the scene, pith helmet at his side.

To while away the late evenings, he walked to the outskirts of town, where he amused himself by shooting flying foxes with long-barreled .303 rifles left over from the Boer War. But his time as a policeman in Rabaul was short. Before the first year of his two-year contract was up, he was dismissed for insolence to his superiors.

Undeterred, he soon found work as a "supercargo" on a trading ship that took him around the islands of New Britain, New Ireland, and the northern Solomons. Supervising the cargo, he would

McKinnon looking over
Alice Springs

regularly "whack" the "natives" with a cane as they loaded the boats with bags of copra, a measure he later insisted was not like "slave-driving and brutality" but "appreciated by the natives [who] . . . were proud of the man who was able to cause them to complete a task satisfactorily."

January 1929 saw the first-ever industrial strike in Papua New Guinea, in which thousands of men stopped work in Rabaul to demand better wages and conditions in the mines and plantations run by their colonial overlords. Only days later, McKinnon sailed for Manila and Singapore, seeking work en route. As his ship left Rabaul Harbor, he lamented the "revolution against the white man" that had been led by native police and Sumsuma, a twenty-six-year-old boat captain. There was even talk among the local population, he said, of "destroying every European in the area." Although the strike lasted little more than twenty-four hours, McKinnon saw it as an indictment of the weakness of Australian administration. As he later explained, "discipline" in Rabaul had "steadily declined," just as it had done with "the Australian natives of the Northern Territory."

In March 1929, he was back in Australia and soon found a job working in a "pick and shovel gang" at Port Kembla Steelworks, before the Depression hit and he lost his position along with thirteen hundred others. Working his way up the coast, he bought an old trotter, "Prince," a saddle, and a bridle and rode toward Queensland, "keeping an eye open for a job." When he received a telegram from the Commonwealth government in 1931—"Glad [to] learn whether you still desirous appointment Police Central Australia, if so advise when prepared [to] commence"—he was working on a dairy farm near Forster on the north coast of New South Wales. Wasting no time in replying, he rode two and a half miles to the local post office to telegraph his acceptance.

Alice Springs in the early 1930s—a "hard drinking town"—was far from thriving. As McKinnon reflected years later, "there was very little in it." People felt isolated from the cities in the south of the continent. Phones were good only for short distances—long-distance calls would not be possible until the Second World War.

Alice Springs from Anzac Hill, circa 1935

Everyday life was lived on an intimate, island-like scale; a few days after McKinnon arrived, he asked where he could get his washing done and was told to "go to Mrs. O'Brien's." On his way there, he passed by Ah Hong's vegetable garden, Wallis Fogarty's General Store at the north end of Todd Street, and the Stuart Arms Hotel on the Parsons Street corner, before lunching at "Kath Rice and Kit Robinson's café," where a "local alcoholic" sat at the end of a long table, "bent forward, with the side of his face resting peacefully in a plate of soup." Opposite the Stuart Arms stood an "old galvanized iron building" and behind it was another "old slab-walled building" that had previously been the general store. Almost every edifice felt temporary, as if the European presence in the town could wither at any moment. The invaders, which included a sizable Afghan community, were vastly outnumbered by "natives," whom they both feared and were determined to displace. McKinnon found Territorians—by which he meant Europeans—"more or less lonely and friendly people."

Kath Rice and Kit Robinson's café, Alice Springs, 1930s

There were only "twenty or so" private residences in the town, among them the thatched-roofed shop of the saddler, Aaron Schunke Meyers, and the nondenominational church of the German missionary Reverend Ernest Kramer. Appointed as missionary to central Australia by the Aborigines' Friends' Association in 1925, Kramer did his utmost to protect, civilize, and Christianize Aboriginal people, professing his stern love—"the blacks," he said, were not to be treated as equals—and making an Arrernte translation of the Gospels. McKinnon remembered Kramer's "wagonette," on which he used to travel "all around Central Australia," "with his family and his goats tagging along behind a coop full of fowls . . . preaching [to the natives]."

In the police yard, there was a makeshift shed that housed "a lock-up store, two or three stables . . . and a blacksmith's shop." As McKinnon recalled in 1981, police records from the department's early days were dumped on the dirt floor out the back. "In the

stables . . . there was a heap, which would have been . . . about 2'6"
high and about 5 or 6 feet across, and this heap consisted of all early
books and correspondence, files and what have you, destroyed by
cockroaches and silverfish and white ants and so on. They were eventually burned and there went what must have been the most valuable
Central Australian records."

Even by the standards of the time, conditions for police were
primitive. McKinnon's supplies consisted of "a bare folding cyclone
stretcher . . . one hurricane lamp, a small room warmer stove, [and]
a table and one chair" to be shared between three constables. When
he asked why there was only one chair, he was told that he could
always sit on his bed. His shower and toilet ("bucket type") were
housed in a tiny timber and corrugated iron shed out the back of the
station. These facilities were also used by Aboriginal trackers and
their families, a provision McKinnon found "disgraceful"; he quickly
succeeded in restricting use of the shed to "constables only." Nearby,
there was a jail with two cells, one for the white man and one for "the
blacks," the latter with an "unroofed exercise yard." Both cells had
"heavy [iron] rings let into the floor" because, as McKinnon insisted,
white and black prisoners "were treated alike in those days."

On the flat, baking red-sand streets of Alice Springs and the
thousands of square miles of "wild" country beyond, the specter of
"the natives" filled the settlers' waking hours and dreams, just as it
had done from the moment Europeans entered central Australia in
the late nineteenth century. Delirious with thirst and hunger as he
explored the region in 1872, Ernest Giles felt "shunned" by Aboriginal people. Although he could see their fires in the near distance, he
couldn't understand why they didn't approach him. "I should greatly
like to catch a native," he fantasized. "I'd walk him off alongside my
horse until he took me to water." Water, of course, was the lifeblood
of the country.

For most Europeans, traveling without Aboriginal guides or

Bed of the Todd River, Alice Springs, 1935

trackers was tantamount to suicide. The first pastoral and Overland Telegraph stations, such as Barrow Creek—the site of a notorious attack by Kaytetye men in 1874, which killed the stationmaster and his linesman and resulted in a wave of reprisal killings—were erected near the water holes of their Indigenous custodians. Tracks that led from the center to the Kimberley were said to be "lined with the graves of unarmed travelers murdered en route." Much of Territory folklore was built on interwoven narratives of settler wrath and vulnerability.

All over central Australia, millennia-old blackfella sacred sites became whitefella outposts virtually overnight. By the early 1880s, "every square mile . . . had been leased or held under application." Yet still the insurgents were forced to yield to Country. While government surveyors marked their maps with the hard, straight lines that separated states and territories, settlers moved through the country from water hole to water hole, their stations, bores, and wells unwittingly following the songlines of the "Seven Sisters" Dreaming that bound central Australia to the rest of the continent.

When McKinnon arrived in Alice Springs in 1931, there were barely more than forty police in the Northern Territory. This minuscule force—renowned for its culture of violence and heavy drinking—was at the center of race relations and had operated under federal government control since 1911, when the Commonwealth assumed control of the Territory from South Australia. Although "native police" no longer existed when McKinnon took up his position, police engaged Aboriginal trackers privately. Poorly paid, they served as "companions," "laborers," de facto police, and "general assistants." Their motivations for taking on the job varied enormously, but almost all of them were lured by the possibility of sharing "in the power and authority of the invader." This included violently subduing their Aboriginal countrymen and -women.

In 1931, Alice Springs was rife with talk of the "wild," "treacherous natives" who "menaced" settlers, evangelists, dingo trappers, and miners in the interior. Some "old-timers" even considered the "blacks" to be "out of control." A five-year drought had exacerbated a slow-burning frontier war and tested the resolve of black and white alike. Prospectors, lured by the stories of massive gold deposits at Lasseter's Reef, "slipped away quietly" into isolated stretches of country for months on end. Like so many of the invaders in central Australia, they were a law unto themselves; the great majority of cross-cultural contact occurred far from the eyes of white law enforcers like McKinnon.

Throughout the Territory, the memory of the Coniston Massacre still burned brightly. That three-month killing spree, sparked by the murder of dingo trapper Fred Brooks, was led by the Gallipoli veteran Constable William George Murray and resulted in the deaths of somewhere between 70 and 150 Aboriginal people northwest of Alice Springs between August and October 1928. Murray, hardened by years of military service and frontier life, was stationed at Barrow Creek, where a memorial served as a daily reminder of the Kaytetye attack: IN MEMORY OF JAMES L. STAPLETON, STATIONMASTER, AND JOHN FRANKS, LINESMAN, KILLED BY NATIVES . . . 23RD FEBRUARY 1874. With a well-earned reputation as a strongman, Murray saw himself as the "protector" of five hundred isolated Europeans who were prey to thousands of "blacks" across central Australia. When he described his dealings with Brooks's alleged murderers, who resisted arrest at Coniston, he made no apologies. Rather than be ambushed himself, he "shot to kill."

Despite the wholesale slaughter around Coniston, Japanangka ("Bullfrog"), the Warlpiri man who murdered Brooks because he had illegally taken one of his wives, escaped Murray's clutches. In a region where a handful of white men regularly looked to Aboriginal women for labor and sex, this was one of the most common sources of conflict. When news of the killings reached Canberra, pressure from humanitarians and the churches soon resulted in Prime Minister Stanley Bruce announcing an official inquiry in late 1928. Stacked with men who were likely to be sympathetic to Murray—like John Cawood, the government resident at Alice Springs, who was also Murray's superior—the inquiry excluded key Indigenous testimony, blithely accepted Murray's implausible argument that he shot in self-defense, and found that the killings were entirely justified because the "natives" were determined to "wipe out the white settlers." As they'd done in the South Australian government's inquiry into killings by the trigger-happy Constable William Willshire—who was eventually found not guilty of murdering two Aboriginal men thirty-seven years earlier—the authorities closed ranks behind their enforcers, refusing to bring them to justice.

In the years to come, McKinnon would get to know Murray

intimately and hear firsthand accounts of "the big shoot up of the Aboriginals" from his Aboriginal tracker, "Police Paddy," who accompanied Murray at Coniston. McKinnon knew full well that the official death toll of thirty-one was a lie, believing it to be closer to ninety. He learned quickly not to speak too loudly about what took place on the frontier. In a culture where local newspapers regularly ran headlines referring to Aboriginal people as "bellicose," "murderous," and "bloodthirsty" "niggers," not to mention the dehumanizing language used to describe young Aboriginal men ("bucks") and women ("lubra" or "gin"), the white man's dispensation of justice was far removed from the letter of the law, which afforded Aboriginal people, as subjects of the Crown, the same protection as other Australians.

McKinnon had entered a brutalized world, similar to the one he had known in Rabaul, where whites commonly assumed that Aboriginal people had to be treated harshly. It was an "us or them" mentality. Whipping, spearing, poisoning, rape, shootings, and long marches of Aboriginal prisoners handcuffed or chained by the neck quickly became part of his everyday existence. "Might is right" and "Fear is the only language they understand" were credos that had marked so much of Australia's frontier experience from the first decades of settlement on the east coast to the blood-soaked invasions of northern Queensland and Western Australia in the late nineteenth century and still applied in central Australia in the early twentieth century. As William Murray remarked in 1933, when justifying his actions at Coniston, "there are times when the natives understand nothing else, as history will show you."

The "killing times" did not end with Coniston, but they did go underground. In the months and years following the inquiry, violent conflict did not suddenly disappear. Although the combined effect of the drought and Murray's punitive expedition now forced many Aboriginal people onto pastoral stations and reserves, there was no lessening of fear in the settler psyche. Sharp divisions of opinion regarding how to "treat the natives" were often marked by a bitter rural/urban divide. While missionaries and humanitarians in the cities described Coniston as a "glaring atrocity" and wondered how it was possible to "regard Australia as a Commonwealth" when its Indigenous people were "detested," "exploited," and "chased" from their country, contributors to newspapers in Darwin lauded Murray as the "hero of Central Australia," a man who had led "the last of the great punitive police raids that alone have made for the safety of the white man in a black man's country." Some even argued for apartheid, like this correspondent from "the never-never," who wrote to the *Northern Territory Times* in May 1929:

> *Winter is here again with his cold nippy winds and bright blue sky and we are making the most of the cold weather while it lasts and milking seventeen cows and storing lots of butter for the season. The stock are splendid and fat and it's a treat to see frisky animals about again. Harry Hentys [sic] murderer is still at large and goodness knows when they will get him. . . . Anyway we can rest assured everything possible will be done to land him now that Constable Murray is on his trail. . . . The blacks are the ruination of the Northern Territory. . . . If the blacks were disposed of the stations in the district would have to employ white labor and why not? . . . All niggers are unreliable, lazy, dirty and not to be trusted— and they are not "cheap labor" as some folk think. . . . The Government should gather up all natives throughout the whole of the Northern Territory and put them away from the whites altogether, why not set apart some waste land. . . . Until the Northern Territory is absolutely free of natives it will never be a civilized state and will never be populated with white Australians as it should. If the Government*

*would only DO something instead of talking so much.
Our motherland would soon bloom and flourish like a
beautiful rose.*

Cheerio, Best Wishes from Mum, Dad and everyone

Many "Centralians" were determined to cleanse the country of any
trace of Indigenous culture. In the early 1930s, the Aboriginal population of the Territory was approximately twenty thousand—nearly
four times greater than the number of Europeans. Believing the
white man's life was "in actual peril," the invaders complained constantly to the authorities that the "Blacks still menace[d] settlers and
travelers in Central Australia." In December 1928, prospector Michael Terry described "an epidemic of cattle killing and unprece-
dented resentment of the encroachment of whites into the almost
deserted interior." He told the story of the well-known station owner
Harry Tilmouth, who was riding along the Lander River when he
came across a young Aboriginal man "armed with kylies and spears."
Enraged at the sight of yet another white intruder, the man shouted
out to Tilmouth at the top of his voice: "This one blackfeller country;
nothing want 'em whiteman; whitefeller shift, can't sit down longa
blackfeller."

McKinnon claimed that things were "settling down" in the area
when he arrived, yet admitted in the same breath that there were still
"disturbances," a thinly veiled euphemism for violent resistance, or,
in his words, "natives attacking whites and whites attacking blacks . . .
and cattle killing and horse killing and sheep killing."

In an effort to curb the violence, the Northern Territory Police
decided to introduce two camel patrols. Albert McColl, another
young recruit recently arrived in Alice Springs, who'd lunched with
McKinnon on the day of his arrival, was placed in charge of the
North West Police Camel Patrol, while McKinnon took the South

West Patrol, which was effectively an area of ten thousand square miles. To assist him, his mentor, Constable Bob Hamilton, "drew a rough sketch of where [he] would be going, showing stations and camps, together with the names of Europeans on whom [he] would call."

Two policemen and their Aboriginal trackers would patrol more than twenty thousand square miles of the Territory. Taken literally, the idea was preposterous. But it demonstrated the authorities' determination to thrust the long arm of the white man's law into every corner of the country. Defining Indigenous resistance as a policing matter enabled the state invasion of Aboriginal lands. His Majesty's government took the land—without treaty, consent, or compensation—and police enforced the theft under the cloak of "law and order."

McKinnon headed out on his first patrol in July 1931, barely four weeks after he had arrived. He was issued "a .44 Winchester rifle, a .45 Smith & Wesson Revolver, stores, and a train of six camels." With him for the three-month journey was "Dingo Mick," an Aboriginal guide who had just been released after serving six months in the Alice Springs jail for cattle stealing. A man who claimed to have rarely "camped out" or cooked anything in his life other than boiled or scrambled eggs, McKinnon would have to learn on the job. As he explained, Dingo Mick would be his teacher. "I was completely at his mercy. He [showed me where to find water] and he gave me my first lessons in cooking damper, even if it did cook in a quarter of an hour and was charcoal outside and pure dough inside. He also taught me that one did not pitch a tent fly to sleep under at night but slept in the open."

It didn't take long for McKinnon to realize that the country was "far different" from what he had "imagined it to be." Years of drought had given way to abundance: "permanent springs and waterholes, rock holes . . . full of pure rain water, claypans . . . holding immense

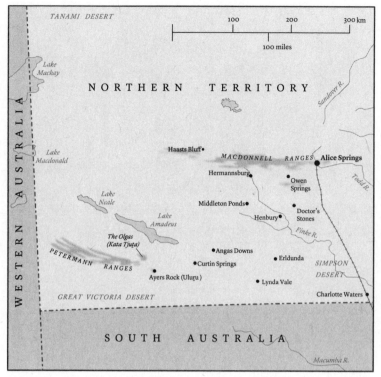

Southwest Northern Territory in the 1930s—McKinnon's patrol area

supplies of water [and] . . . wells on every station" that he visited to replenish his "meat supply." He saw hundreds of wild camels, horses, donkeys, and feral cats roaming the country. They disturbed the soil, consumed native wildlife, denuded vegetation, and fouled water holes. McKinnon's concerns, however, were different. "They're in such vast numbers," he said, "they interfere with the feed that should be there for the cattle."

As he moved about, he met prospectors whom he'd known when he worked in Sydney and western New South Wales, and others with whom he'd sailed to Vancouver. A shifting tide of single men moved across the country, looking for work, adventure, and wealth. Meeting them on his patrols, McKinnon felt that he was in touch with a

F. J. (Dutchy) Waalkes, Bill McKinnon, Bob Buck, Doug Fuller, "300 miles southwest of Alice Springs, in about June 1933"

network of roving "mates"—or, as he described his method of befriending others, he "mated up."

He also encountered men who reveled in the isolation. On July 21, at Glen Helen Station, he met the owner, Fred Raggat, "an Englishman and one of the first settlers in the area," who "lived [alone] in a big, dark, one room building with two doors but no windows." During all his travels in the early 1930s, McKinnon would meet only one white woman on a cattle station. Because she was alone for up to six months at a time, he gave her a small pistol for protection.

His other lifeline was mail. He corresponded regularly with his family back in northern New South Wales, especially his brother, James, who was a policeman in Mullumbimby. After seven weeks on patrol, he received his first letters from his family. They'd been flown to Hermannsburg—established as a Lutheran Aboriginal mission in 1877—then brought to him by a station hand on horseback. Around the campfire, he read newspapers and letters that were already more than two months old. Some of his letters to his brother—many of them long, frank reflections on the travails of his life in inland Australia—were passed on by James to the local Mullumbimby newspaper, where they were published under the matter-of-fact headline THE DAILY ROUND OF A POLICE OFFICER.

Alice Springs, Northern Territory, 4th October, 1931

I have just returned from my first patrol, and had a very decent trip—was away eighty five days. I saw plenty niggers, some friendly, others not friendly, but had no trouble whatever. They are treacherous here, not like the New Guinea boys. . . . On my next patrol, I am going to follow the prospecting party, right out to the Rawlinson Ranges, on the Westralian border. There is one stretch of 100 miles without water. I will cover this in four days, which is quite easy for camels. I will have two 10-gallon canteens of water, which without stinting myself, will last me five days. . . . I expect to see plenty uncivilized natives out there.

For readers in the more settled districts in the east, central Australia was an exotic curiosity. *The Mullumbimby Star* proudly claimed McKinnon as one of their own, boasting that he'd been selected from a field of more than seven hundred men who had applied for his position as a policeman. At the height of the Depression, Australia's unemployment rate was one of the worst in the Western world. Back in Alice Springs after nearly three months on the road, McKinnon wrote again to his brother, explaining that he would remain there at least until the Christmas racing carnival, when people "came from hundreds of miles around," and the federal election on December 19, 1931, as he would soon be "doing a few hundred miles in the Police car handing out postal voting papers to the residents in the back blocks." In January 1932, only weeks after Joseph Lyons, leader of the newly formed United Australia Party, defeated Labor prime minister James Scullin, McKinnon was out on his next patrol.

Frustrated by his Aboriginal tracker—"the laziest and most useless specimen I have ever come across"—he was determined to find a replacement who knew all the water holes on the way to Ayers Rock (Uluru), the Olgas (Kata Tjuta), and the Petermann Ranges. It was here, in country that was deemed less suitable for cattle, that Anangu elders remembered being herded into the South West Reserve, created as a "sanctuary" by the government in 1920, and which included Uluru and Kata Tjuta. McKinnon knew he was entering an area that few Europeans had seen. Of all the places in the country that he passed through during his first months on patrol, it was Uluru that stayed with him. When he saw the rock for the first time, he was awestruck, spending most of his daytime hours trying to capture its majesty on film.

On the long journey there and back, he read avidly. Entranced by Ion Idriess's *Lasseter's Last Ride*, which told the story of Lasseter's Reef—the prospector, con man, and fabulist Harold Lasseter died alone in the Petermann Ranges in January 1931 after an aborted mission to find the mythical deposits of gold—McKinnon wondered if "the Lasseter hoodoo" would descend on him too. Finding the cave where Lasseter, "dying from starvation," "lay in hiding from the hostile natives"—Lasseter was actually kept alive for weeks by Anangu— he soon found himself in an equally precarious position. The camel that carried his water canteens bolted. After trying for an hour or more to catch him, he drew his rifle and shot the animal from afar, killing him but at least saving his water. In searing heat, assailed by "swarms of ants and flies," and still several days' travel from the nearest water hole, he decided to return to Alice Springs. With only one "useless" camel left and haunted by the prospect of "hostile natives," he feared he might not survive.

"Looking out from inside Lasseter's cave in the Petermann Ranges, Feb. 1932"

When he arrived back in Alice Springs, he developed the photographs he had taken at Lasseter's Cave and Ayers Rock. Aware that he was following in the footsteps of the early explorers, and seduced by the rock's beauty, McKinnon fancied himself a new kind of trailblazer: the policeman photojournalist. He sent his photographs to *The Queenslander*, a major Brisbane newspaper, which published them promptly in a full-page spread. They included a "general view of Ayers Rock," "rock-holes of water," and "Aboriginal drawings in one of the caves in Ayers Rock." The centerpiece was a photograph of

McKinnon, standing beside the trig erected by W. Gosse

McKinnon himself, standing in white trousers and pith helmet like a latter-day Livingstone "on the summit," close to the pile of stones originally left by William Gosse sixty years earlier.

Many years later, cataloging his personal archive, he was keen to place himself in the pantheon of explorers: "Ayers Rock—found and climbed by explorer W.C. Gosse on 20.7.1873. Next climbed by Alan Breaden and David Oliver in March 1898, who placed wax vesta tins in the trig erected by Gosse. Climbed by W. McKinnon on 19.2.1932, and again in 1933 and 1935. At Breaden's request in 1933 I looked for and found his wax vesta tin and returned it to him." The one photograph that he chose not to send to *The Queenslander* in 1932, the strangest and most memorable of all, is the shot he took of himself taking "a bath" in a rockpool on the summit, his clothes piled behind him at the foot of the cairn.

The publication of McKinnon's photographs reflected the growing public fascination with the rock that rose mysteriously "out of the [desert] sand" and his personal ambition to be both the center's law enforcer and its storyteller. McKinnon was intrigued by the drawings he'd seen on the cave walls at Uluru. Occasionally, he even paid "old [Aboriginal] men" with a "bag of flour" to perform corroborees for him. Like so many of the station owners he was employed to protect, he was convinced that the "blacks" would never develop the country, but his extensive travels had brought him moments of contemplation, at Uluru and elsewhere, when he became faintly aware of the depth and complexity of Aboriginal culture.

Although he had taken to his new job with unbridled enthusiasm, he was disappointed to lose one of his closest mates, fellow patrolman Albert McColl, who was transferred to Darwin in May 1932. He had relished swapping stories with McColl when they returned to Alice from their months-long patrols, just as he'd done with geologist Cecil Madigan, to whom McColl introduced him. McKinnon and Madigan quickly became friends and corresponded. Madigan

McKinnon "having a bath in a rock hole at the very top of Ayers Rock," 1932

sent him a copy of *Central Australia* in 1936, an account of his epic journey of exploration by camel, which McKinnon treasured and, to his lifelong regret, lost six years later, when Japanese forces launched two devastating bombing raids on Darwin. But it was not only his friendships with Europeans that sustained him.

Most of his time on patrol was spent in the company of his Aboriginal trackers, and he was astonished by their skills: "We'd come across some tracks and the trackers would look at them and they'd say: 'oh that one belong so-and-so, that one here.' 'When were they made?' 'Oh, that one bin makem yesterday, or might be two moon' and so on. They could follow tracks the same as we could read books . . . it was truly amazing." His two longest-serving trackers—the ominously named "Carbine" and the much-feared "Police Paddy"—had both grown up at the Lutheran mission at Hermannsburg. Paddy, together with William Murray, had been responsible for much of the killing during the Coniston Massacre. He and Carbine taught McKinnon to cook goannas—they tasted just like "flathead fish"—feral cats, turkeys, and kangaroos. Alone together for weeks on end, they shared meals, stories, and laughter. But there was never any doubt who was in charge.

In the spring of 1932, after Reverend Ernest Kramer reported the discovery of the bodies of an Aboriginal "mission boy and his wife," "375 miles west of Alice Springs," McKinnon set out with two trackers to apprehend the killers. At a water hole near Haasts Bluff, he came upon a tribe of more than one hundred Pitjantjatjara, two of whom claimed to have witnessed the "killings." "Through an interpreter," they explained that the killings were "double-revenge," a payback exacted for the killing of an Aboriginal woman the previous summer. Trekking more than one hundred miles over sandhills, the police were led to the bodies of the victims. McKinnon proceeded to "exhume" and "examine" the bodies, "preserve the heads," and take them with him as evidence. As he explained later: "I had the job of digging them up—only a bit over a foot deep—and as we had to in those days, remove the heads and [take them] back to Alice. We used to have to produce the heads of murdered people to prove to the courts that they were dead." Over the following weeks, he traveled south, moving through the Petermann Ranges, then east, toward the Finke River, before finally heading north. Living mostly on "rabbits and damper," he arrested seven Aboriginal men who were allegedly responsible for the killings.

Their journey back to Alice Springs was already punishment of a kind. Tethered to camels and "handcuffed together" in relentless summer heat, the men walked hundreds of miles in torturous conditions. As McKinnon told a journalist on his return, it was "the worst journey" he ever undertook. He preferred the more "humane" method of chaining his prisoners by the neck—which allowed "complete freedom of movement"—a measure that had recently been banned in the Northern Territory but would return in October 1935, when police were allowed to use "lightweight" neck chains until the practice was finally phased out in the 1940s.

> The natives have been amenable, and have done some remarkable stages, two 45-mile stretches in one day. Owing to the order that we are not to chain the natives, very much against my grain I was forced to use the only other method—handcuff them to a tree during the night. Anyone with experience of natives must realize that handcuffs in hot country infested with flies and ants are nothing but torture. [Among the accused is] Prenty . . . a notorious leader of this band of killers which, according to natives, has terrorized the far west country for some years. Four years ago, while serving a sentence for cattle spearing at Alice Springs, he broke jail, and was tracked for 50 miles south by a police boy. He was shot in the elbow with a rifle and was sent to hospital at Port Augusta.

This was typical of frontier justice. Police seeking to find those responsible for one killing saw no harm in rounding up "troublemakers" of all kinds.

Two months after his departure, after traveling thirteen hundred miles, McKinnon arrived in Alice Springs, carrying the heads of the two Aboriginal victims in a kerosene can. Three of the seven Pitjantjatjara men he arrested had managed to escape. Miraculously, the other four men were alive. In January, the victims' skulls were exhibited in a Darwin court, together with the spears allegedly used in the killings.

Despite predictable challenges translating and clarifying evidence, the judge reminded the court that the accused were being tried under British law and were "entitled to all the privileges under that law." The defense counsel persuasively argued that his defendants were "not familiar with the white man's ways," and the jury found the accused "not guilty." Once released, the men began their arduous return journey, walking hundreds of miles back to their country. McKinnon's efforts had come to naught. Police like him and William Murray—who, four years earlier, had failed to see the two men he'd arrested for the murder of the trapper Brooks convicted—were frequently frustrated by the difficulty of securing convictions in the courts.

Three months after McKinnon's prisoners were set free, he heard from Darwin that his colleague Albert McColl had been speared to death on Woodah Island off the Arnhem Land coast. "We were both in Darwin," he recalled later. "We went up there for [the] Supreme Court, and he went in from the Roper River and we came back on the train. Well, he got off the train at Mataranka and that was the last time I ever saw him. He was speared on the first of August 1933." It was a blow McKinnon felt keenly; he had lost a colleague and friend, and there were surely times when he wondered if the same fate would befall him.

In June 1933, Albert McColl had set out from Darwin with a police party to arrest the murderers of five Japanese fishermen who were speared to death in Caledon Bay in September 1932. He was the first member of the Northern Territory Police Force to be killed by "natives." As soon as the telegram was sent confirming his death, newspapers ran hysterical headlines—SAVAGE ABORIGINES; [CON-STABLE] SPEARED THROUGH THE HEART BY BLACKS; WILD NORTH NATIVES AMBUSH POLICE—many of the articles syndicated from Darwin and Brisbane, where the mood quickly turned to "seeth-ing . . . indignation." GOVERNMENT PREPARES FOR PUNITIVE EXPEDI-TION AGAINST BLACKS. EQUIPMENT TO BE RUSHED NORTH. MASSACRE OF WHITES IN ARNHEM LAND FEARED. LESSON MUST BE GIVEN, ran one headline.

In the Territory, McColl's murder and the death of the Japanese fishermen fueled fears that Arnhem Land, an Aboriginal reserve and "the last remaining stronghold of the Aborigines," was out of control. To allow the murderers to go unpunished would be to "destroy the fear of the police among the Aborigines." Ernestine Hill, one of Australia's most popular writers, who knew McColl personally, described his death as a "ferocious slaying." Arnhem Land was almost impregnable, she claimed. "In the twentieth century, it harks back to the night of antiquity."

It was impossible to imagine a wider division between the "settled south" and the "wild" north. When he heard of the plans for a punitive expedition, McKinnon wrote to his superiors in Darwin offering his services—"I volunteered. McColl was my mate." Much to the dismay of many in Alice Springs and Darwin, the decision to send an expedition in response to McColl's murder rested with Canberra. It was a federal problem.

With the memory of Coniston still fresh, the government's decision quickly became the focus of international attention. As the new Lyons cabinet deliberated, letters of protest—from unions, feminists, church groups, humanitarians, communists, Australian Labor Party branches, the Australian Federation of Women Voters, and the British Commonwealth League and the Anti-Slavery Society in London—rained down on the government. Telegrams were sent warning of the "slaughter of innocents," while letter writers registered their disgust, calling on the government to prevent "loss of life." Within three weeks, Lyons, increasingly alarmed by the clamor of national and international protest, claimed that his government never had "any intention of sending a punitive expedition." Although supplies of ammunition and equipment requested by the Northern Territory administration had been shipped to Darwin, Lyons insisted he had no idea "how the word punitive crept in."

The protests had stayed the government's hand. As humanitarians celebrated, correspondents to northern newspapers angrily denounced Canberra's alternative plan—a peaceful party of missionaries that would bring the murderers to justice—condemning the Yolngu as a "cowardly thieving, worthless race." Some correspondents wrote poems, pillorying the "Canberra mugs" who lacked the courage to endorse the one remedy that would work: "the mighty roar of powder and the hum of killing lead." The days of the isolated frontier—out of sight, out of mind—were coming to an end. Like many others in the Territory, McKinnon could see that the new era of federalism and rapidly expanding communication networks meant that the actions of police and settlers in central Australia were being scrutinized in every capital city and internationally. It would not be long before he, too, became the subject of a national inquiry.

McKinnon (standing, far left) with his "prisoners" at Bob Buck's station at Middleton Ponds. Women and children related to "prisoners" in the front row. Buck (standing, far right). The arrested (unidentified, shirtless) men stand in the back row to McKinnon's left. Police Paddy kneels, center row, second from left.

3

DUST AND BULLETS

On August 30, 1934, already out on patrol and moving through some of the "filthiest" country he'd seen—"solid walls of dust, all round, all day"—McKinnon was tasked with tracking down those responsible for the death of Kai-Umen, an Aboriginal station hand about twenty-five years of age, near Mount Conner, fifty miles east of Ayers Rock. McKinnon, a frequent visitor to Angas Downs Station, where Kai-Umen was employed, had known him for nearly three years and considered him "quite civilized." He had been executed by a group of fellow Pitjantjatjara men for infringing tribal law. The following morning, at a nearby camp, McKinnon arrested two men, Numberlin and Wong-We, but not without difficulty. As soon as Numberlin saw McKinnon coming for him, he ran into the bush "armed with two spears and a woomerah." McKinnon and Carbine gave chase. "Carbine brought him down with a well-aimed stone that struck him on the back of the head." When another suspect threatened to attack Carbine with his spear, "Carbine promptly bashed him with a piece of wood making a deep cut over the eye." At the same time one of the others bolted. Paddy chased him and fired six shots with the rifle, while McKinnon "fired two long pistol shots," but he got away.

Once Aboriginal people were classified as "suspects" or "prisoners," McKinnon, Paddy, and Carbine had no hesitation in using any means necessary to intimidate and apprehend them. For the next few days, they continued their search for the rest of Kai-Umen's "murderers." On September 7, at a nearby camp, they "rounded up and disarmed between forty to fifty natives"—McKinnon did not explain how—before arresting Paddy Uluru, Yokununna, Joseph Donald, and another man, Toby Naninga (also known as Walpaku Ngulunytju, "Frightened by the Wind No. 2"), on murder charges. He also "secured" Kai-Umen's wife, Judy, as a witness. By the time he had questioned "suspects" and made the arrests, he was convinced that Kai-Umen had been choked and beaten with stones and sticks by a group of at least seven men, led by Numberlin and Nangee, the second of whom he had not yet arrested. They had done this, they confirmed, because Kai-Umen had broken tribal law.

It was now McKinnon's job to assert the invaders' law over and above the dispensation of justice already carried out under tribal law. The killing had occurred within his jurisdiction. When he crossed the border into South Australia a few days later and learned that a European employee at Tieyon Cattle Station had stabbed two Aboriginal men, killing one in "cold blood," he took no action because it was the responsibility of South Australian police. On September 30, fifty days after Kai-Umen's death, McKinnon was led to Elangilla Hill near Mount Conner, where he found Kai-Umen's "dried body" decomposing under a thin covering of "grass, mulga branches and stones." He took his bearings and further "statements from [the] prisoners," including Judy's testimony that the body was indeed Kai-Umen's. He then followed standard procedure, securing the head with the aid of a shovel, then photographing the remains and returning them to the earth. One week later, at Middleton Ponds, holding and turning Kai-Umen's skull in his hands, he heard "something rattle inside." A "bullet fell out." He promptly interrogated every prisoner, threatening to beat them if they refused to cooperate. Within minutes, he had secured a confession. Two of the men had allegedly used a dingo trapper's gun to kill Kai-Umen.

At "piccaninny daylight" on October 8, 1934, McKinnon was woken by his tracker Police Paddy. The six Aboriginal prisoners he'd arrested for Kai-Umen's "murder" had escaped. McKinnon was furious. "All hands sprang to it immediately." Paddy and Carbine set off on foot without food or water, searching for tracks and carrying a .44 rifle. McKinnon would catch up later with the camels. Within twenty-four hours, at nightfall, the trackers returned, lighting their way through the scrub with firesticks, hungry and desperate for water. The drizzle that had fallen throughout the day had not been enough to leave even a small pool in the rocks. The next morning, McKinnon, Paddy, Carbine, another Aboriginal man, pastoralist Bob Buck, station hand Bert Branson, and Barney, whom McKinnon had arrested for possession of stolen goods weeks earlier, set out after their "quarry." Hampered by severe storms, which erased the escapees' tracks, they were forced to camp near a stand of desert oaks in the sandhills.

They had covered fifty miles in rough, mountainous country, and everyone was so stiff from the constant jogging of the camels that no one could move without excruciating pain. On the third morning, the party rode into a nearby property and replenished their supplies of meat and bread, before heading for Inindie Soak in the Kernot Range. Nearing the hills, McKinnon decided to dismount and tie the camels up, approaching on foot for the last mile in case the animals could be heard. They found the soak dry, but going farther up the gully they discovered a cave with small fires that were still warm.

McKinnon felt certain the prisoners had camped there the previous night; the remains of a small kangaroo they had eaten were scattered on the ground.

Convinced he was on their trail, he tallied up the remaining food and found he had only enough left for three men for a week and no certainty of water in the near future. It was then that he decided to send "Buck, Branson and their Aboriginal back." He would continue with Paddy, Carbine, and Barney, who had plodded on dutifully behind them, tethered to a camel. The next day, Carbine showed McKinnon the tracks of the six men they were chasing. They were quite distinct. Traveling in single file, each man had placed his feet "right in front of the tracks of the man in front of him." They appeared to be headed for Ayers Rock.

An early capture now seemed likely, but the country they were moving through continued to push them to the breaking point. McKinnon flogged the camels to keep them going. Over the following days the animals began to show signs of distress through hard traveling and shortage of food. But McKinnon was thrilled when they came across another campsite—the fires were still quite hot. He sent Paddy to climb a nearby hill and take a careful look around. Seeing the escapees' tracks and realizing they were not far ahead, Paddy thought he could arrest them on his own and immediately took off in pursuit, leaving McKinnon and Carbine to push on alone.

At nightfall there was no sign of Paddy, nor of Barney, who for the first time had failed to catch up to them. Making camp, McKinnon realized that their water supply was so low that he and Carbine would have to go to bed without a mouthful to eat or drink. It was a miserable night. On the fifth morning, they managed to extract some water from a "salty native well," but it was so deep that it was impossible to give the camels a drink. Carbine could see that the escapees had drunk from the same well. McKinnon was now certain that he would catch them before sundown. After traveling only four miles, they were surprised to see Paddy coming toward them with two prisoners, Numberlin and Wong-We.

Angry with himself for not giving clearer instructions to Paddy, McKinnon was frustrated to learn that he had singlehandedly raided the escapees' camp the previous evening. Although he had arrested two, the four others—Paddy Uluru, Joseph Donald, Toby Naninga, and Yokununna, the last of whom Paddy had wounded—were still on the run. If it were not for the fact that Barney finally appeared a few hours later, carrying the last of their beef and flour, they would have spent another night without food and with little water. The incredible strain of the journey was testing McKinnon's resolve. For a moment, he was so enraged he felt like taking it out on Paddy—"I felt that I could do anything to him."

Knowing that he was so close to the escapees made his frustration even harder to bear. He decided that the best option was to direct Paddy—together with Barney, Numberlin, Wong-We, two camels, and a riding horse—straight to Ayers Rock, where they would wait for him and Carbine. After sending them on their way, McKinnon and Carbine headed for the campsite Paddy had raided nearly two days earlier. Once there, the trail of Yokununna's blood made it easier for them to track the four remaining escapees. They quickly realized that they had split up in an effort to foil their pursuers. Undeterred, McKinnon pushed his badly suffering camels over huge sandhills, continuing to whip them constantly to ensure they kept a brisk pace. Exhausted, he and Carbine pulled up briefly at dusk, in a depression between two sandhills. They shared what food they had with a quart pot of tea and then pressed on into the night. There was no point in stopping now.

At 11 p.m., they were only two miles from the rock. Dismounting from the camels, lest their cries be heard, they moved on foot through mulga scrub. It was impossible to see a track. For McKinnon—who walked straight into trees or stumbled over stumps or timber on the ground—the experience was a nightmare. Much to his relief, they eventually came to a halt about a quarter of a mile from the rock and tied the camels to a tree. He told Carbine about the hole of beautiful water he remembered on the northwest side of the rock from a previous trip. They walked on, carrying a quart pot in great anticipation.

But on arrival they found the hole was dry. Carbine immediately began digging in the sand, and when he'd reached about two feet down he finally struck water. No matter how much McKinnon drank, he felt that his thirst would never be quenched. He went back to get the camels but found they'd already broken loose and headed toward the hole themselves. When he returned they were lying, parched, in the bottom of the empty soak. By now, it was well after midnight and they decided to turn in. On the morning of Saturday, October 13, they were up and traveling by 7 a.m., heading for "Maggie Springs" (now Mutitjulu Waterhole) as heavy storm clouds and thunder rolled overhead.

As soon as they arrived, Carbine jumped and called out, "Yokununna track." Pointing to a single faint track on damp ground, he hurried off to the southern side of the rock while McKinnon searched the huge heaps of broken rock and caves near the spring. Within ten minutes torrential rain began to pour. He already knew the rock well enough to know that this was a rare event. As the rain pelted down, a great sheet of water cascaded off the rock, the heavy wind gusts whipping it into fine spray as it fell, penetrating into the caves. It was a grand sight.

In the space of fifteen minutes, the rain had stopped and the spring was dry again. In those few minutes, the camels "drank and drank and drank." McKinnon kept watch at the spring while Carbine continued to scour southward. At noon he heard a shot ring out. Hurrying around, he could see Carbine standing above him on a piece of broken rock. He told him that he'd spotted Yokununna from behind and fired at him when he'd refused to surrender.

McKinnon—already incensed by the escape and weeks of pursuit in difficult terrain—was closing in on his prey.

I had been searching for about five minutes in the rocks, caves and tunnels, when on bending at the entrance to a cave I smelled a decidedly Aboriginal odor from inside. I heard a scramble and caught a glimpse of Yokununna. He could not understand English so I called his name several times hoping he would come out. The next thing I knew, a stone hurtled past my head, close enough to feel the draft created by it. He rushed further in, dropped on his side and wormed his way into an inner tunnel through which the light was showing. When only his feet and legs were showing I fired a pistol shot near his feet but he kept going. Rushing in after him I placed my left hand on the side of the entrance and, bending down to see the position another stone thrown by him struck me on the knuckle of my left index finger, crippling the hand for the time. Taking a quick glimpse I saw him facing me and picking up another stone. Keeping my head clear, I pointed the pistol in his direction without taking any aim whatever, and fired a second shot. I called out again as I had been doing, but got no response, and could hear nothing. I did not know whether he was armed with any native weapon or whether I had injured him. I called Carbine, who came up to me.

While I covered the tunnel with my pistol Carbine spoke in his dialect and (as I struck matches) went in. He said "Yokununna come out." (Carbine squeezed in sideways and saw Yokununna sitting with his head fallen forwards on the ground. He told him to "get up" and Yokununna said: "You leave me here I want to stop.") Carbine and I then carried him into the open and saw that he was badly injured. We had just commenced the task of carrying and lowering him a distance of about 40 feet to the ground when Police Paddy arrived with his party. Prisoner Barney came up and assisted us to lower Yokununna to the ground. The day was now very hot and steamy, and a gale of wind was blowing. We picked a comfortable position in the shade and sheltered by long grass, where we laid Yokununna. He spoke in his dialect. I said to Carbine "What is he saying?" He replied "him talk—me like die now." Yokununna frequently called for "cuppie" which means water, I personally took him a drink whenever he called for it, and the trackers did what they could to make him comfortable. At about 3 pm I took the prisoners to the waterhole for a drink, and when we returned Yokununna was dead. I superintended the digging of a grave and we buried him.

Yokununna's death stilled the frenzy of the hunt. That afternoon, October 13, McKinnon recorded the events in his patrol logbook, which he later edited and typed up: "Attempted to rearrest Yokununna at Ayers Rock. Shot him in self-defense and in attempting to prevent further escape. Yokununna died three hours later. Buried body. Separate report furnished." Exhausted by the effort of chasing the escapees to the rock, his food "almost finished," McKinnon quickly made the decision not to continue the search for the remaining men (Paddy Uluru, Joseph Donald, and Toby Naninga).

On the morning of October 14, he set out on the one hundred miles of dry stretch from Ayers Rock to Angas Downs Station, then on to Buck's station and Middleton Ponds, where he arrived five days later. He conducted further arrests on his way, including that of Nangee, whom he claimed to be Numberlin's main accomplice in the killing of Kai-Umen. On November 25, he finally reached Alice Springs with a party of twenty, including three prisoners—Numberlin, Nangee, and Cowarie—the last of whom, like Wong-We, was later released because he had not used the rifle to kill Kai-Umen. More than three months after McKinnon had exhumed the body, Kai-Umen's mummified head was still wrapped in his "pack saddle" as he dismounted his camel in the police yard at Alice Springs.

Two weeks before McKinnon arrived back in Alice, the high court overturned the conviction and sentencing to death of Dhakiyarr Wirrpanda, the Aboriginal man arrested for the murder of McKinnon's former colleague Albert McColl. Within twenty-four hours of his release in Darwin, Dhakiyarr had mysteriously disappeared, possibly killed by police or white vigilantes angered by his release. As McKinnon digested the news of the court's decision upon his return, he was about to discover that a markedly different conception of the law was closing in on the lonely life of a patrol officer in the interior. Now, back in Alice after months on patrol, his dogged pursuit of Yokununna would soon be scrutinized by the distant eyes of Prime Minister Joseph Lyons's government in Canberra.

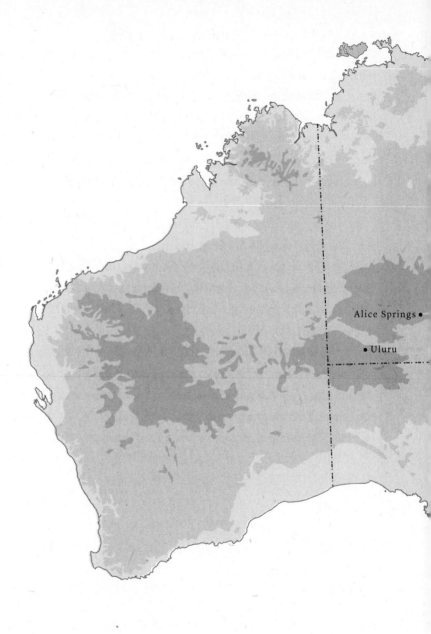

Alice Springs •

• Uluru

Kilometers

0   250   500   750   1000

Miles   310   620

Topographic map of Australia

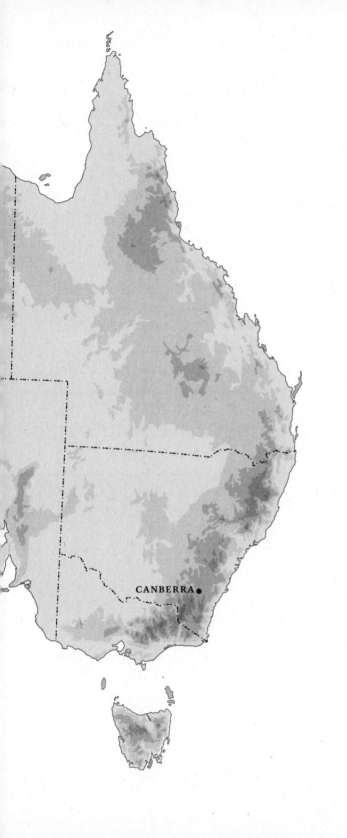

CANBERRA

N

4

A DOMAIN OF
THE IMAGINATION

When non-Indigenous people imagine Australia whole, with Canberra as its seat of federal parliamentary government and law, we see it from above. Mapped. A meandering line that encompasses 3 million square miles of the earth's landmass, creating a shape and form so familiar it needs no explanation.

On a satellite image, the internal state borderlines we've drawn across the surface of the world's only island continent disappear. The populous edges thicken and shimmer. The center dominates. Reaching out. An ocean unto itself. From an aircraft, the center of Australia appears infinite. A country "beyond the edge"—unfathomable, humbling, and eternal—a country for disappearing into. The plains and hills stretch all the way to the horizon, beating in a blinding haze of ochre and red. Even the perpetual groundswell of heat fails to dim the echo of the vast inland sea that once covered central Australia, more than 150 million years ago. The forces that sculpted the country have left their ineffaceable mark. Every gibber plain and desert in the arid heartland is haunted by the memory of salt water.

Climbing "the summit of a sandy undulation" in 1844, the

explorer Charles Sturt gazed out on "interminable" ridges of sand dunes that extended "northwards in parallel lines beyond [his] range of vision." They appeared to him "like the waves of the sea." The center of Australia was once imagined by Europeans from the deck of a ship. In 1770, when James Cook sketched his first maps of the continent as he sailed up the east coast, he sprinkled mountains like confetti onto the blank spaces of the interior, as if they might crown verdant valleys and grasslands. For the countless Europeans who followed in Cook's wake, the coast quickly became the center of "civilization," while the vast unexplored lands of the country's interior remained an enigma.

To find the center was to confront the metaphysical dilemma of being a white man in an Aboriginal country. As the explorers set out on their quest, they wrote their awe, terror, and incomprehension onto the country they encountered—a godless landscape of "wretched bareness" where there were "no Sundays." Biblical images of trial and suffering abounded. In 1844, Sturt, unnerved by the "solemn stillness" and "monotonous wilderness," felt himself "the last of creation amid the desolation and destruction of the world." Forced to relinquish his dream of an inland sea and driven back by exhaustion and lack of adequate food and water, Sturt believed that it was his destiny to find the center of Australia and "unfold the secrets of the interior."

For Ernest Giles, travel into an area seemingly more distant and foreign than Europe or North America was an existential journey into "the center of silence and solitude." To reach this almost mythical place, it was necessary to "walk off the map."

In April 1860, John McDouall Stuart, the obsessive and fiercely independent Scot who had accompanied Charles Sturt in 1844, found what he believed to be the center of Australia around 124 miles north of present-day Alice Springs. Climbing a nearby hill, from where he could see a "large plain of gums, mulga and spinifex, with watercourses running through it . . . but no water," he "built a large cone of stones" and attached the British flag to it. Near the top of his cairn, Stuart, as if marooned on an island, placed a "small bottle," which contained his message to any future passersby. His note remained undisturbed for twelve years before it was discovered by James Ross, one of the workers on the Overland Telegraph Line (completed in 1872), and in 1905 found its way to the State Library of South Australia, where it remains today.

To confirm possession of hundreds of thousands of square miles—an area several times larger than his homeland—Stuart wrote a note of fewer than one hundred words. He dated the letter, noted that the British flag had been raised, stated his name and address, however approximate—"about 2 miles South, South West at a small Gum creek"—and placed his signature at the bottom, together with that of his second-in-command, William Kekwick, and their eighteen-year-old companion, Benjamin Head.

The center of the continent was finally inscribed with the presence of white Australia. It was a startling dismissal of the rights of Stuart's fellow British subjects—more than ten thousand Aboriginal inhabitants of central Australia. As Stuart wrote ominously in his journal, the lonely flag he had planted on the hill was "a sign to the natives that the dawn of liberty, civilization and Christianity [was] about to break upon them." It happened much as Stuart predicted. Soon to come were pastoralists and their thousands of cattle, missionaries with their gospels and psalms, government officials, educators, judges, and law enforcers—like the policeman Bill McKinnon.

Looking closely at Stuart's missive, you can see that the phrase "Center of Australia" is underlined. This was his goal, after all: to find the center. It's only natural that he wanted to emphasize his achievement. But perhaps he was also trying to convince himself that he had truly found the center.

As he looked across a waterless plain from the top of the hill that would eventually be named in his honor, he might well have wondered what exactly he had found. The closer he came to the center, the more it dissolved. Cavernous silence. Immeasurable landscape. Draining heat. A country that would almost take his life. But he had his measurements. In order to calculate the center of the continent, he had taken his latitude from the angle of the sun: "Today I find from my observations of the sun, 111° 00" 30', that I am now camped in the center of Australia. I have marked a tree and planted the British flag there." It appeared at the time to be a sound calculation. Except that Stuart's "center"—commemorated by the erection of a cairn in 1960, which remains a tourist stop on the Stuart Highway today—is no longer considered to be the center of Australia.

In the 1930s, Australian geologist and explorer Cecil Madigan journeyed by camel through central Australia. Like anyone game enough to venture into what he called "this vast, lonely inland region," Madigan could not escape Stuart's legacy. No stranger to the travails of exploration, Madigan had already traveled to the Antarctic—a "different desert"—as Sir Douglas Mawson's meteorologist in 1912–13.

In 1929, he'd also taken part in the first reconnaissance flights across Lake Eyre and central Australia. Like so many who would follow him into the interior, Madigan surveyed the country by plane before he tackled it on foot. Pictured at Marree, clad in his finest tweed as one of his Afghan cameleers watches on, he exudes an unmistakable air of gentlemanly authority.

Promotional photos aside, Madigan's immaculate appearance would not be maintained en route. Like Stuart, he was on a personal quest to place his name on the honor roll of Australian explorers, and in 1939, he became one of the first Europeans to cross the desert he'd named after the geographer, industrialist, and washing-machine baron Alfred Simpson, a feat he achieved with nineteen camels and a party of nine in merely twenty-five days. By then, he was a regular visitor to Alice Springs and a "firm friend" of Constable Bill McKin-

Cecil Madigan,
Marree, 1933

non, who fondly recalled Madigan's dust-blown figure appearing in the police yard with his "string of camels" laden with geological specimens to take back to Adelaide. The two men bonded as they exchanged stories of their treks.

In 1933, 124 miles north of Alice Springs, Madigan was keen to examine Stuart's method of finding the center of the continent. As he well knew, "the term center of Australia has no exact meaning without further explanation." The center of such "a large, irregularly-shaped area" could be calculated as the farthest point from the coastline, which, as it turned out, was little more than six miles from Stuart's cairn. Or it could be found by identifying the center of gravity, or the midpoint between the extremes of latitude and longitude, or simply estimated as an area rather than a precise place.

While Madigan was pleasantly surprised to find that Stuart's calculation was "quite near the point most remote from any part of the sea shore," he was equally convinced that Stuart had merely found the "point that looks like a center." In his determination to "fix" the center, Madigan decided to find "the center of gravity of the area." He proceeded to cut a map of Australia from a piece of "thin sheet metal" before dangling "a lead weight on a string across its face hundreds of times." The result? "The center of gravity of the surface area of Australia," Madigan confidently asserted, "found by cutting out a map and suspending it from several points together with a plumb bob . . . is about . . . 257 miles south of Central Mount Stuart." Almost twenty years earlier, the US Coast and Geodetic Survey had used a similar method to identify the geographical center of the United States, suspending a "cardboard cut-out" map of the United States from a piece of string and rotating it to find the centroid—the point at which there is equal volume on all sides.

Madigan's centroid proved to be remarkably accurate despite his crude method. It was only eleven kilometers west of the Lambert Gravitational Centre of Australia, established with the aid of advanced technology in 1988 and commemorated by the erection of a triangular stainless steel frame—a miniature replica of the flag mast that crowns Canberra's Parliament House.

Not that Madigan was wholly satisfied with his efforts, given that the position of his center of gravity appeared to be an uninhabited moonscape. Surely the center of any country was settled? Alice Springs, Madigan reassured himself, "remains the [true] center of the continent, the capital of the Center, in splendid isolation." By the 1930s, Australia already had more centers than it required.

Few Australians realize that Central Australia has also existed as a political entity. In the mid-nineteenth century, the colony of South Australia stretched from the southern end of the continent all the way to its northern coastline. The area north of the twenty-sixth parallel (the northern border of South Australia today) was originally known as the "Northern Territory of South Australia." In 1911, the

Commonwealth government assumed responsibility for the entire northern region. In 1926, keen to divide an area that was thought too large to govern, the federal government passed legislation (enacted in 1927) to create two separate jurisdictions: the territory of "Central Australia," with Stuart (later Alice Springs) as its capital, and the territory of "North Australia." When the Depression hit and finance for separate administrations became harder to justify, the Scullin Labor government decided in 1931 to fold Central Australia and North Australia into one jurisdiction: the Northern Territory. The short-lived political entity of Central Australia swiftly returned to its stateless existence: a domain of the imagination.

While the explorers strove to demonstrate knowledge of the country by mapping precise coordinates—crossing from one end of the continent to the other, establishing "lines" of movement and communication across the deserts, and demarcating properties, states, and territories from one another—the true center eluded them. The longer and harder they searched, the closer they seemed to come to their own demise.

Sturt was forced back by lack of water, his eyesight permanently damaged; Stuart, almost crippled by "infantine weakness," was carried out on a stretcher; Giles imagined the "eye of God" looking down on him in a "howling wilderness" and, crazed with thirst and hunger, devoured a "tiny" wallaby alive at dawn—while his traveling partner, Alfred Gibson, was confounded by a country in which only Aboriginal people knew how to survive.

Their accounts of their journeys spoke of torturous ordeals and heroic failure. They were unable (and frequently unwilling) to recognize the country's supple, interconnected, Indigenous heart—etched as it was in the songlines of millennia. What they imagined as determinate was fluid. What they saw as empty was layered with story. Nor could they appreciate the abundance of the center: water in tree hollows and roots, wild passion fruit and oranges, native figs, bush tomatoes, bananas, coconuts, and plums, and the sweet nectar of the honey grevillea. Nor its beauty: flocks of iridescent green and yellow budgerigars, vividly colored parrots, kingfishers, finches, chats and wrens, striking desert bloodwoods, ghost gums and river red gums, and a vast array of seasonally flowering plants. Where European explorers saw arid desolation, Aboriginal people knew a larder teeming with sources of animal protein and fat and a wide variety of plants that provided nutrition, medicine, tools, and shelter.

At the abandoned Dalhousie Springs Station, a hundred miles north of Oodnadatta, the panels that interpret the station ruins tell of the tragedy that colonization wrought for all concerned. When construction workers from the Overland Telegraph Line "discovered" the springs in 1870, there were around four hundred to six hundred Lower Southern Arrernte and Wangkangurru living nearby. In 1901, only three decades after the station homestead was built, their population had declined to fewer than two hundred. Years of drought, competition for water and hunting grounds, and the 1919 influenza epidemic further depleted their numbers. By the 1930s, the homestead was abandoned, as many pastoral properties were amalgamated. Faced with yet another drought and the financial crisis caused by the Great Depression, almost all the European workers departed, leaving Aboriginal stockmen to manage the country around Dalhousie. Despite the dislocation of their communities, Aboriginal people worked the stations and maintained their connection to the land.

In their hunger for productive earth, the pastoralists and workers had crossed "Goyder's Line," yet another imaginary border, which, from the early 1870s, marked the northernmost point where annual rainfall (twelve inches) was considered sufficient to support European-style agriculture. A few good years enticed them farther north; a few bad years broke them. Today, driving the trail of the white man's tears into the center, it seems that the country has dismissed every attempt to conquer it. As climate change pushes Goyder's Line ever southward, it's impossible not to wonder how long it will take before the blazing heat and drifting sands claim the Overland Telegraph Line and every ruin left standing. Perhaps this is the deeper source of white melancholy. Alone in the immense antiquity of the landscape, everything Europeans have constructed appears ephemeral—faint static in an ocean of Indigenous knowledge. The center remains Aboriginal Country.

In 1983, when British writer Bruce Chatwin confronted the "horror" of Alice Springs—a town he described as "a hornet's nest of drunks, Pommie-bashers, earnest Lutheran missionaries, and apocalyptically-minded do-gooders"—he slowly came to realize that beneath the thin, hardened surface of European settlement lay the "Aboriginal Dreaming tracks, [something] so staggeringly complex, and on such a colossal scale, intellectually, that they make the Pyramids seem like sand castles." But how to write about them, he asked, "without spending twenty years here?"

Alongside whitefellas' metaphysical quest for the center and the insubstantiality of their settlements was the dawning awareness that Indigenous cultures and the Country that gave them life possessed eternal qualities that were both material and spiritual. Trekking alone through central Australia in the late 1970s, Robyn Davidson saw this clearly: the "big spaces and possibilities"—"limitless," with their roots "more in the sub-conscious than the conscious"—spaces she saw as "metaphors for other things"; ambiguous and elusive.

No other place in the center embodied these metaphorical dimensions more than Uluru.

When Europeans first came upon Uluru, they often searched in vain for the language to describe a place they found incomprehensible. Neither words nor images seemed to do it justice. To set eyes on the rock was to be silenced. While convinced from the first moment that Uluru was among "the most majestic wonders of the natural world," they lacked intimate knowledge of its Indigenous custodians, the Anangu, and the visitors struggled to convey the deeper emotions they felt in the rock's presence.

From the moment of first European contact in October 1872, when the explorer Ernest Giles saw the rock from a distance, and nine months later, when William Gosse climbed "the most wonderful natural feature" he'd "ever seen" and named it Ayers Rock after South Australia's five-time premier, Henry Ayers, visitors were overwhelmed by its remarkable isolation. It could be seen "clear and distinct" from as far as forty miles away. William Tietkens, who took the first photograph of Uluru in July 1889, remarked on the "graceful curves and lines" draped down the rock's side, which he thought resembled "an enormous curtain turned into stone." Anthropologist Baldwin Spencer, who led the Horn Scientific Expedition to central Australia in 1894, made a hurried twelve-day side trip to spend just thirty-six hours with "one of the most striking objects in Central Australia." After journeying for so long to reach it, and confronting what he called its "lonely grandeur," Spencer sensed that it held deeper truths about the country itself.

For countless others who followed, it was impossible to turn one's eyes away from Uluru. Like the Chartres and Ely cathedrals in France and England, it rose above the plain; one immense rock, "splitting the horizon like the temples of an ancient city." Its mammoth proportions had a natural symmetry. "Regularly domed," it appeared to be sculpted with "architectural precision." Every part of its surface was rounded and "almost polished." Foundations and walls climbed "perpendicularly on either side for over 1000 feet."

Visitors walked around its perimeter like tourists moving around the outside of Canterbury or Notre-Dame, searching for a photographic angle that might capture its magnificence. The rock's caves were like side altars, their walls and ceilings decorated with sacred

Uluru, 2013

ancestral drawings. Late in the day, the rock's color shifted constantly, deepening in the afternoon light from pale rust-orange to incandescent Venetian red. It was a legendary place of teaching and learning—the meeting point of the Aboriginal people and songlines of central Australia and beyond—a place of contemplation and worship that rested alone, "like some huge cathedral" in the desert.

It's staggering to contemplate that the landscape Aboriginal people saw thousands of years ago "looked much the same as it does now." Geologists believe the sand dunes of the center have remained in their present position for approximately thirty thousand years. Uluru's monumental "arkose"—"a coarse-grained sandstone rich in the mineral feldspar"—was formed more than 500 million years ago.

Of the hundreds of thousands of Australian and international travelers who visit Uluru every year, few can dispense with the maps that appear instantly on their phones and computers and see the country through the eyes of the Anangu. Like everywhere else in Australia, the roads we travel on and the imaginary lines drawn by the Commonwealth to divide state and territory jurisdictions overwrite an intricate network of Indigenous cultures and languages. Of the three main language families that span the desert region of central Australia, those of the Western Desert comprise the largest language group in Australia. They include Pitjantjatjara, Luritja, Yankunytjatjara, and Pintupi, all of which are spoken in the Mutitjulu community near Uluru and throughout southern central Australia. For the Anangu, Uluru is inseparable from Tjukurpa, or traditional law, a body of knowledge that is largely kept secret from outsiders.

"Mutitjulu" translates literally as "belonging to Aboriginal people." Home to the Anangu at Uluru, it's also the name of a water hole at the southern end of the rock. It was here, in 1934, that Europeans' awareness of Uluru's sacred significance emerged in tandem with the gruesome reality of White Australia's incursion into central Australia.

Bill McKinnon was another seeker of the center. While I'd known of his story for many years, once I asked myself what had happened in his life before and after the shooting, everything changed.

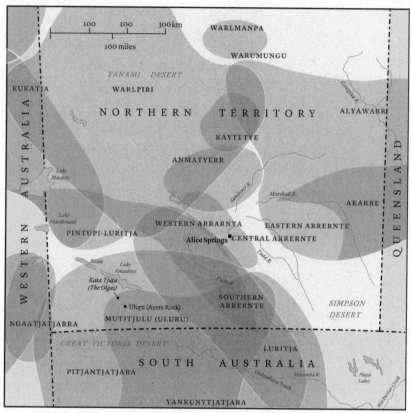

Aboriginal languages, central Australia

PART TWO

INVESTIGATIONS

Bill McKinnon and Doreen Taylor's honeymoon site at Simpsons Gap

5

COMMONWEALTH OFFICERS

The months following McKinnon's return to Alice Springs after shooting Yokununna would prove momentous in more ways than one. In December 1934, he married Adelaide-born Doreen Taylor, with whom he would spend the next four decades of his life. They met through Doreen's sister, Nance, who was a teacher at the Alice Springs school. Eighteen months earlier, shortly after they fell in love, McKinnon had been out on patrol. At Cowlers Soak, not far from Dashwood Creek, around 125 miles west of Alice Springs, he made camp, pulled out his logbook, and wrote down the two opening and two closing lines of "Lone Dog," by British poet Irene Rutherford McLeod.

> I'm a lean dog, a keen dog, a wild dog and lone,
> I'm a rough dog, a tough dog, hunting on my own;
> Oh mine is still the lone trail, the hard trail, the best,
> Wide wind, and wild stars, and hunger of the quest.

Transcribing these lines fused his desire for Doreen with his craving to become a legendary figure in the history of central Australia.

Bill McKinnon and Doreen Taylor, 1934

The following day, he wrote again, only this time with more conventional sentiment: "Oi dunno why we took a walk, / Oi dunno where we went . . . / Oi only know we came back 'home / Together on the bus, / An' all the world was makin' love— / Or was it us?" What Doreen made of these ballads from her lone hunter is difficult to say, if she ever set eyes on them. They honeymooned at Simpsons Gap, thirteen miles west of Alice Springs. McKinnon, typically, recorded the dimensions of their tent. "Doreen & I spent our 'honeymoon' weekend there under a pitched 10 × 12 ft. tent fly."

McKinnon's first months of married life coincided with an inquiry that would threaten to derail his career. Until now, like every policeman in the territory, McKinnon had served as both police officer and protector of Aborigines: "You'd be their protector," he recalled, slightly bemused, "and yet you'd go into court and prosecute them." In a Commonwealth territory that was poorly resourced, police, pastoralists, and missionaries constituted the arms of the state. Under the crucial piece of legislation—the Aboriginals Ordinance (1918; amended many times subsequently)—police enforced a range of laws that directed and constrained Aboriginal people's lives. They were not allowed to drink alcohol or possess firearms; nor were Aboriginal women (officially) allowed to cohabit with white men.

Alone with his trackers for months on end in isolated country, McKinnon was virtually the "sole moderator" of cross-cultural contact and conflict. He distributed rations, visited missions, took the census, assumed custody of "half-caste" children, and transported them to institutions like the notorious Bungalow in Alice Springs or others in Darwin. This practice was given extra force shortly after the Commonwealth assumed control of the Territory in 1911, and forcefully pursued under the direction of Cecil Cook, who, in 1927, became the Territory's chief medical officer and chief protector of Aborigines. McKinnon arrested Aboriginal people for petty crimes and, of course, for murder, even if these killings occurred because of the exercise of tribal law. Police and trackers—both white and black—had been doing this since the late nineteenth century. He also deterred prospectors and dingo scalpers—lured by government bounties, many of them were "coming up from South Australia . . . by car and camel"—from entering Aboriginal reserves, arresting and fining those he met on his patrols who had trespassed into lands set aside exclusively for those termed a "remnant race."

Race relations in the Territory continued to be fraught. Throughout the 1930s, newspapers across the country ran sensational headlines regarding the fate of white settlers in northern and central Australia—MURDERED BY BLACKS; NATIVES FIRE ON POLICE; PASTORALIST'S SKELETON FOUND—while humanitarians rejected the waves of white hysteria by pointing out that the shooting of Aboriginal people was commonplace: NATIVES SHOT: WHITE MEN'S SPORT. While the language was scandalous, the pastoralists' fear and vengeance were real. The Commonwealth government sanctioned the conquest of central Australia but left the task to a handful of outnumbered intruders, missionaries, and police, many of whom claimed that the humanitarians had no idea of the dangers they faced. They also worked hard to disguise the extent of the violence they employed to secure their foothold in the country.

Like the station owners, the miners spreading through the Territory relied on Aboriginal labor, without which settlement was impossible. Interstate papers carried reports of "slave-like conditions in Northern Territory mines" and deaths of Aboriginal workers. Administrators and lawmakers debated whether British law should prevail over Aboriginal customary law in every circumstance, some supporting the idea of "native" courts. Anthropologists eager to study the vestiges of a dying culture rounded up and examined Aboriginal people as if they were curios rather than human beings. Missionaries sought to bring in lost souls from the wilderness as they carved up the country with their own imperial gaze, some, like Alice Springs' first resident Catholic priest, Father James Long, claiming godly jurisdiction over a "bush mission" that covered the entire Northern Territory.

For every European, whether pastoralist, policeman, priest, scientist, or prospector, to talk of the distance traveled was to spread the word of the white man's conquest of the interior. As McKinnon wrote at the end of his patrol journal on returning to Alice Springs in late 1934: "Total. 121 days. 2181 miles. Certified correct." The recollection of the miles traversed reeled the country in, layering it with stories of unbearable hardship and agonizing struggles for survival. Yet all the while they feared their foothold was tenuous. The growing "half-caste" population, fathered by single white males and born to Aboriginal women, who were usually left with the offspring, was already creating concern about the future racial composition of the Territory. Europeans lamented that in some places beyond Alice Springs it was impossible to find a "pure" white child. It was in this climate of racial anxiety that the Territory's small number of administrators and settlers sought to combat what many of them saw as unnecessary interference from an ignorant Commonwealth government regarding their cruel treatment of Aborigines.

In early January 1935, as the inquest into Kai-Umen's death was about to get underway, McKinnon and Carbine returned to the grave site with Victor Carrington, coroner and deputy administrative officer of the Territory, and William Kirkland, acting chief protector of Aborigines and acting chief medical officer. The final day's travel through the sand was horrendous. They were forced to break new roads and shift timber for miles, eventually giving up on their vehicles and walking the "last 1 and a half miles to view [the] body." Unlike Kirkland, who'd only arrived recently in the Territory, Carrington was very well-known to McKinnon. He had presided over his marriage to Doreen at the Alice Springs Registry a month earlier. As was so often the case in the Territory, personal and professional loyalties—mates investigating mates—undermined the capacity of the law to get to the truth of the matter. Standing for the second time over Kai-Umen's grave, McKinnon photographed his headless remains. Tending his archive years later, he captioned the macabre image: "Deceased Aboriginal's body being removed from the ground. And to think I used to grill kangaroo steaks on this shovel blade!!"

The first real test of McKinnon's account of events came in February 1935, when he gave evidence in court during the subsequent trial, which was also the inaugural sitting of the Northern Territory Supreme Court in Alice Springs. In evidence presented to the inquest, Numberlin had allegedly confessed to borrowing a dingo trapper's gun to shoot kangaroos and using it instead to shoot Kai-Umen. Now, in court, Numberlin and his accomplice in the killing, Nangee, both pleaded not guilty.

After Kai-Umen's "mummified head"—marked by two entry wounds and one exit wound probably caused by a .22-caliber bullet— was held up in the courtroom and identified by his widow, McKinnon told the court how he'd initially arrested six Aboriginal men, all of whom admitted to participating in Kai-Umen's execution, before they escaped and headed toward Ayers Rock, where he shot Yokununna: "He resisted arrest and I shot him in self-defense, and while attempting to escape from custody."

When McKinnon took the stand, he was confronted with damning evidence regarding his professional conduct. For the inquest into Kai-Umen's death, McKinnon's colleague, Constable Bob Hamilton, had taken statements from Police Paddy and several of the Aboriginal people McKinnon had arrested, including Numberlin and Nangee, Paddy Uluru, Judy, and Cowarie. Police Paddy—whom McKinnon would later describe as "a full-scale rogue and a drunk in town, but . . . worth his weight in gold in the bush"—told Hamilton that McKinnon had slapped and kicked Numberlin before extracting his confession. But Beecher Webb, counsel for the defense, knew much more about McKinnon's brutal methods. After McKinnon had given his version of events, Webb wasted little time in grilling him:

WEBB: Is it correct that the natives would not answer your
    questions regarding the shooting, and that you picked up
    a packing instrument and flogged Numberlin?
McKINNON: It certainly would not be. I have never shown
    any physical violence to the natives.
WEBB: Is it a fact that [station master Bert] Branson sooled
    [sicced] dogs on to two unconscious natives?
McKINNON: Not to my knowledge.
WEBB: Why did you shoot Yokununna?
McKINNON: He was in a cave with a low, narrow entrance. I
    called him several times to stop. A stone flew past my
    head, and another hit my hand.
WEBB: How did you know he was there?
McKINNON: I smelled him, and the tracker tracked him.
WEBB: When Paddy and Carbine went out to find Nangee,
    did you know that another native had his arm broken?
McKINNON: I did not hear it there.

WEBB: Have you ever ill-treated a native named Wong-We or another called Salt Peter while in custody on this occasion?

McKINNON: I did not.

WEBB: If there are scars on the backs of the two prisoners, will you deny that you caused any of them?

McKINNON: I will.

Webb's line of questioning was so vigorously pursued that Judge Thomas Alexander Wells was forced to remind him that McKinnon was not on trial. Although his caveat would have chilled McKinnon: "If it is thought that the suggestions made against him are worthy of putting him on trial for some offense, it will, no doubt, be done."

For Numberlin and Nangee, there was little hope of explaining their involvement in Kai-Umen's death to the court. Numberlin spoke little English, and Nangee's comprehension of the language was limited. Sydney Walker, the interpreter, told the court that Kai-Umen had "breached tribal law" by revealing secret knowledge "which must not be explained to women." "Numberlin and Nangee," he argued, "were ordered to kill Kai-Umen by the elders of the tribe, and they had to carry out their instructions. They would not have decided to do it of their own accord." If they had not done so, he insisted, "they would have been killed" themselves. The jury was only partly persuaded, finding the two men guilty but recommending "mercy on the grounds of tribal law." Judge Wells deferred sentence for a week "to enable the defense to secure evidence about a certain secret tribal ceremony," yet in the same breath he reflected sarcastically that "some of these anthropologists may be of use . . . they always seem to be where they are not wanted, and never where they are wanted."

Wells was clearly ill-disposed toward any suggestion that the accused were following their law in killing Kai-Umen: "Such men no doubt stick to customs when it suits them. . . . I think personal spite had a lot to do with it." As he handed down his verdict, sentencing Numberlin and Nangee to ten years in prison, he reminded the court that it would be wrong to "allow men to commit offenses of this sort and get off scot free." "We do not want to hang them," he proclaimed, "and the only alternative is imprisonment. If undue leniency is accorded them the effect on other Aborigines is likely to be bad."

Newspaper reports noted that "the sentence was not explained to [Numberlin and Nangee], who had obviously not understood their long trial." As Webb asked the court pointedly during the trial, "Why prosecute them for breaking laws they did not understand?"

Even before Judge Wells sentenced Numberlin and Nangee, the Commonwealth government was deeply troubled by Webb's allegations of McKinnon's cruelty toward the Aboriginal men in his custody. Less than three weeks after the first reports of the trial appeared in the press, the Department of the Interior in Canberra wrote to the Territory's deputy administrator, Carrington, with some urgency, asking him to send all the information he possessed relating to the allegations against McKinnon.

It was at this point that things began to unravel. Until he received the request from Canberra, Carrington had planned to do nothing about the allegations. Their disclosure, he argued lamely, might have prejudiced the chances of a "fair trial" of Kai-Umen's killers. Having received a request from his superiors, he had little choice but to gather and forward all relevant information regarding McKinnon's alleged mistreatment of Aboriginal prisoners. A fortnight later, in early March 1935, the Commonwealth read further statements from McKinnon's prisoners and other informants collected by Webb and Kirkland, including damning accounts given by Numberlin, Nangee, Barney, and Wong-We. In his evidence submitted to the inquest into Kai-Umen's death, McKinnon stated on several occasions that both he and Police Paddy had "cautioned" the prisoners during the course of their inquiries. Now, after further investigation, it became abundantly clear that "cautioned" was a thin disguise for brutal treatment. For the first time since Kai-Umen's death nine months earlier, the voices of some of the men McKinnon arrested could be heard. The stories they told—of McKinnon and his trackers handcuffing them to trees, of him kicking and punching them, whipping them with bullock-hide ropes and chains, beating them with camel irons until their blood flowed and their limbs were broken, and depriving them of food and water—sent shock waves through the department in Canberra. McKinnon's trackers, Carbine and Paddy, were responsible for some of the most degraded behavior. Paddy had "tied a rope around [one prisoner's] legs and dragged him along the ground." Then he pulled off his trousers and urinated and defecated over his face. Like Carbine, Paddy was accused by some who gave evidence of him sleeping with their women.

After Carrington mailed the statements to Canberra, he wrote again about Olive Pink, the Sydney University anthropologist and fierce advocate for Aboriginal rights who, weeks earlier, had pleaded with Thomas Paterson, minister for the interior, for "real justice." "You have no idea," she told him, "how abominably little fair play" Aboriginal people received. In late February, after she'd read reports of the trial in Alice Springs, Pink also wrote to her friend and colleague John Cleland, pathology professor at Adelaide University, eager to start a "fighting fund" to assist Webb to "bring McKinnon 'to book' & imprisonment & . . . dismissal for the murder of [an] unarmed . . . native . . . on an Aboriginal Reserve (as Ayers Rock is)." Incensed that the very man who was supposed to be the "Protector" of Aborigines had shot and killed a "suspect" armed with "stones," she was determined to prod the authorities into ensuring that justice was done. Pink was fearless and she was convinced that McKinnon was lying. Carrington, however, thought her a meddling do-gooder who "unjustly criticizes and harasses police officers" and would be better "kept away from Aborigines." Then, as if to forestall what he knew would be a vigorous response from the Commonwealth once officials had read the statements from the Aboriginal men, he affirmed McKinnon's innocence: "I consider that there was neither carelessness in the escape [of the prisoners] nor culpability in the shooting. The matter would not have arisen had neck chains been in use."

Carrington's explanation carried little weight in Canberra. By early April, the government, embarrassed by the publication of lurid stories of McKinnon flogging Aboriginal prisoners, and determined to put an end to the image of a lawless center beyond the Commonwealth's control, announced a board of inquiry, which was formally appointed by Governor-General Sir Isaac Isaacs on May 8, 1935.

While Carrington and the Commonwealth were corresponding regarding the allegations against him, McKinnon was temporarily stationed at the Old Telegraph Station at Charlotte Waters, 168 miles south of Alice Springs. When he received word of the inquiry, he followed instructions and drove immediately to the nearest railway station, fourteen miles away. Despite the serious allegations against him, his rugged appearance was embraced enthusiastically in the Territory press: "Fifty miles back along the line at Abminga when the south bound train drew in, the lights from the carriage windows fell on a figure in khaki, Constable W. McKinnon of the Northern Territory police, standing beside the travel-stained truck in which he and his wife, formerly Miss Doreen Taylor, of Adelaide, had driven from Charlotte Waters."

The khaki-clad lawman had received instructions to travel to Alice Springs and attend the first sitting of the Commonwealth inquiry "into allegations of cruelty by him to natives" and his shooting of Yokununna. Listening to ABC radio, McKinnon heard the names of the board members who would sit in judgment on him: John Cleland (chairman), professor of pathology at the University of Adelaide, who also had a keen interest in anthropology, botany, and ornithology; Vin White, recently appointed assistant chief protector of Aborigines in the Northern Territory; and Reverend John Sexton, Baptist preacher and secretary of the South Australian Aborigines' Friends' Association. Charles Mountford, amateur anthropologist, was to serve as the board's secretary, and Ted Strehlow, the brilliant linguist who was only weeks short of his twenty-seventh birthday, was to be special adviser on Aboriginal languages and culture. Six days before the inquiry was announced, Strehlow lamented the indifference to Aboriginal culture displayed by so many of his contemporaries: "If only White Australia would realize . . . the riches of the wonderful heritage, which it is throwing to the wind & treading under its feet, much could be done & saved." The government's appointment of the inquiry implied a profound change: the lives of Aboriginal people mattered as much as those of any other Australians.

The question of how British law could accommodate Aboriginal tribal law had been a burning and unresolved issue for many years. A key Commonwealth report into the "condition" of Aboriginal people in central and northern Australia handed down in 1928 by John Bleakley, Queensland's chief protector of Aborigines, recommended that "so called Aboriginal criminals should only be tried by a special tribunal of experts on Aboriginal customs and laws." Like Bleakley's enlightened recommendation for the establishment of a "native state with self-government," his call for special tribunals went largely unheeded. In May 1934, the Commonwealth minister for the interior, John Perkins, issued an ordinance stating that "native law or customs" be taken *into consideration* when sentencing Aboriginal "murderers," but the final decision remained with judges. The board of inquiry into the shooting at Uluru was forced to confront the failures of the policy of "protection" on several fronts. Its composition, at least, was promising. It was certainly a more independent board than the one established in 1928 to inquire into the Coniston Massacre. And it would also make an effort to gather evidence from many Aboriginal informants. From the outset, McKinnon was adamant that he had nothing to hide, telling a journalist before he boarded the train to Alice Springs that he was disappointed to learn the inquiry would be conducted in private: "I have nothing whatever to conceal," he vowed, "and I would have preferred that everything said at the inquiry should be made public."

Long before the inquiry was underway, it was clear that McKinnon was far more concerned than he let on. On May 14, at Abminga Station, he handed a personal letter to Thomas Paterson, who would soon be appointed as the new Commonwealth Minister for the Interior and was fortuitously visiting the Territory for the first time, attaching his typed-up "Story of the Escape of Six Prisoners."

> *I respectfully ask permission to hand you this file unofficially unless you wish to make use of it. I am simply showing you a little bit of what a man in the Northern Territory Police Force is likely to go through and, having gone through it, to be met with, as you know, the prospects of an Inquiry as an outcome of the experience. Any remarks I have passed I say with respect, and at the same time I assure you of my loyalty as a member of the Northern Territory Police Force at all times.*
>
> *W. McKinnon. Constable*

McKinnon attempted to take the initiative. His account of the shooting would be passed on by Paterson to Cleland and the board, just as he intended. In the interview he gave to the Queensland journalist, he again went on the front foot with a combination of outright denial and special pleading: "If the authorities attach significance to the stories by outside members of the public who know nothing about the Aboriginal question, their purpose in policing this back country will be defeated," he said. "I have been a friend of the blacks. I am prepared to challenge Mr. Webb or any other person to do a trip through my South West Patrol District under ordinary circumstances and then say the police camel patrol is merely a holiday trip, with no responsibility or risk. . . . Anyone who thinks the task of a single white policeman in securing prisoners and evidence and bringing them to headquarters intact is a holiday has a strange idea of recreation." McKinnon, who insisted that his prisoners' escape and Yokununna's death "were the result of the authorities' refusal to provide chains and reliable locks," appeared to be trying to preempt the inquiry. Four weeks later, he was reprimanded by A. V. Stretton, superintendent of police, who reminded him that "considerable embarrassment may be caused [to] the Government and the Minister by Constables granting interviews to press representatives." McKinnon replied immediately, denying that he had "spoken" the words quoted by the journalist. In his logbook, he simply noted the facts of the matter: "25 May 1935, left by private car at 11am to Alice Springs to attend Board of Inquiry . . . into allegations of cruelty by me to Aboriginal prisoners & to decide whether shooting of Aboriginal by me at Ayers Rock was justified. Traveled all night."

On May 27, the board held its first session in Alice Springs. While the hearings were not open to the public, news of the inquiry was advertised by notices posted around town. Three days later, its members were on the move. Over the next month, they traveled through the interior, gathering evidence at locations as far afield as Hermannsburg and Ayers Rock. The novelty of a mobile inquiry—its distinguished cast driving (and pushing) trucks and cars up sandhills, riding camels, and taking evidence at campsites, roadsides, and wherever necessary—amused journalists, who were transfixed by the image of a court held "under the stars." McKinnon, who of course knew the country, and where and with whom certain evidence might be found, traveled with them as the accused, guide, and cook. Bizarrely, the board, which was to inquire into the allegations made against McKinnon, welcomed him as a fellow traveler. His side of the story—he conducted his own defense—was their daily bread.

McKinnon, left, standing with Bob Buck at Middleton Ponds Station, June 1935

Five days after leaving Alice Springs, on June 4, the party arrived at Middleton Ponds, where they found the fabled station owner Bob Buck. Buck had been made famous by Ion Idriess in the bestselling book *Lasseter's Last Ride*. It was Buck who searched for Lasseter, found and buried his body somewhere "in the beyond," and returned with his notebooks. The trickle of white men, like McKinnon, who dropped by Buck's station often dreamed of entering "the history books," perhaps for discovering "lost treasure" in the "wild" interior, or, as Reverend John Sexton put it, by gathering up the stories of "stone age man." Buck's station buildings on the banks of the Palmer River were "tucked up against a large sandhill," as if they'd been dug in for added protection. In the journal he kept along the way, Charles

Middleton Ponds Station, June 1935

Mountford described his host's dining room as looking "like an armory." One wall was "practically covered with all kinds of firearms, revolvers, rifles and shotguns, all rusty looking and dusty." Buck had erected a shrine to weaponry—his house, itself designed to repel Aboriginal attacks, was stocked with an arsenal large enough to defend Alice Springs. Every bed in his place "had a formidable looking revolver at the foot."

From Middleton Ponds, they moved on toward Angas Downs Station. But the going was so tough that teams of donkeys were needed to drag the old Chevrolet truck "across the sandy bed of the Palmer." Trying to motor up drifting sandhills was a disaster. "Because of the continuous gear work," the motor overheated, and the "boiling oil was sprayed all over the floor boards and the occupants of the cab as well." They were forced to push the vehicles as much as drive them—the Chevrolet was bogged nineteen times in the first eleven miles.

By the time they reached Angas Downs the decision was made. Sexton, Branson, Constable Hamilton, and Police Paddy would stay behind. Leaving the vehicles and taking the camels with them, Cleland, Strehlow, White, McKinnon, Carbine, interpreter Sydney Walker, and Mountford would go ahead to Ayers Rock. The slower pace and easier going afforded more time to appreciate the country. On their way, they passed through "beautiful glades of desert oaks" burrowed between the sandhills. The country was bursting with color—blazing red soil, "the green of the flowering plants and young spinifex," the "black trunks of the desert oaks"—all of it "backed by a sky of the deepest blue."

Mountford, intrigued by the gibber plains, "which [appeared] like a closely packed mosaic . . . as if they had been coated with varnish," photographed them incessantly. Daily chores, however, continued to be a struggle. Adding soap to brackish water only created a "thick sediment" that made it impossible to wash their clothes or themselves.

Camp dinner, possibly at Owen Springs (McKinnon, middle right), 1935

Pushing the Chevrolet

Mountford complained of feeling "sticky all over," his hair standing on end "like a wire brush." When the water in his canteen went "bad," he dosed it with Worcestershire sauce, "which, though it burned [his] mouth, disguised the disagreeable taste." At night, temperatures fell to well below zero. Wash water "flung away after breakfast froze on the ground."

Perhaps to distract them from their discomfort or perhaps to ingratiate himself in the hope of earning their sympathy, McKinnon told stories of his adventures in the center as they sat around the campfire. Several days earlier, evidence had been collected from "certain Aboriginals" who testified that McKinnon had given two men a "hiding" at Hermannsburg Mission. The inquiry would later learn that he had "flogged" two others.

On the morning of the fourteenth, everyone woke at dawn, eager to reach Ayers Rock before sundown. Mountford and Strehlow were already under the rock's spell. After a "beautiful sunrise," Mountford could see it looming "red in the distance, the caves and great gutters on its side now showing up distinctly." Strehlow, who loved the freedom and independence of camping out—"my home is wherever my camels are and my gear"—caught his first glimpse of the "goal of his boyhood dreams," "shimmering in a dim almost transparent hue of light blue sky on the southwestern horizon." It was as if they were journeying to the Holy Land.

After riding for the entire day, they crossed the last sand ridge "about an hour after dinner . . . and had, for the first time, an uninterrupted view of the rock." Mountford struggled to find the words to "describe its beauty or its size." "As we drew near the scene," he reflected, it "became more imposing. The walls rose a thousand feet above us, the rim standing out in strong relief against a sky, turquoise in color and flecked with dainty cirrus clouds." The cathedral was slowly coming into view. As they set up camp at Maggie Springs, their bunks only a few yards from a wall of rock "nine-hundred feet high," Strehlow could feel the presence of "the great silence of eternity." "All hushed tonight; only the moon is shining down upon the great black walls of rock—and one feels that the Land of God is indeed near." Barely able to contain his excitement, Mountford borrowed a lamp and rushed to visit the caves nearby. Like Baldwin Spencer in 1894, he wanted to "copy the native paintings on the walls," but once he entered one of the caves, the weight of its history came down upon him.

> It was a strange experience sitting in that cave. The lamp was continually going out, and in the darkness one felt dissociated from everything that was real. It seemed as if I were surrounded by the presence of those who for untold centuries had frequented this cave, painted their strange symbols on the walls, and conducted their secret ceremonials. I wondered what would happen if one of the aboriginals belonging to this spot were to come upon me. Would he attack me as an intruder, which he had every right to do, or would he treat me with the courtesy which they so often extend to strangers? Everything was so still about me, not a single sound. From where I sat I could look through an

opening in the tumbled rocks and see the moon sailing along in a clear sky, for the feather like clouds of the afternoon had gone, and the lower rim of the full moon was just skimming the edge of the great mass of rock above me. A single square of moonlight lit the ground a little distance from where I sat, accentuating the darkness around me. I stayed in that spot, sitting in the dust of ages of occupation, until quite late, returning to camp to spend a restless night, fitfully dreaming of the aborigines and the cruel treatment accorded to them.

The grim reality of the purpose of the board's visit kept rubbing up against the lure of the rock and the "dust of ages" of Indigenous "occupation." Convinced that his God had "fashioned" the "great Rock," Strehlow was unable to forget that it was "the body of a dead man" that had brought them here, just as Mountford, gazing up toward "a small rock crevice a few hundred feet" above his head, could all too easily imagine Yokununna's "tragic and unwarranted death."

The moment they arrived, McKinnon and Carbine went with John Cleland and Vin White to the spot where the shooting took place. McKinnon stood in front of the entrance to the cave where he had fired at Yokununna and demonstrated what had happened. Thus, some of the first detailed sketches and photographs of Uluru were created in order to document the shooting of an Aboriginal man. The white man had come again to take his measurements in the center of the continent.

The following morning, Cleland and White watched as McKinnon exhumed the body. For Strehlow, it was unforgettable: "[I] saw the scene of the final tragedy to-day. I was greatly shocked at the way in which poor [Yokununna] met his death—a poor hunted creature, shot callously at least twice in the cave, without being able either to defend his life or to escape. And now he is being taken back—his bones and head wrapped up in a calico parcel; his vitals, lungs, blood, entrails, liquefying flesh in a large billycan. And that is permitted by our white man's civilization." What he saw that day would shape his views on the application of British justice in Aboriginal Country for the rest of his life.

With the grisly job of exhuming the body done, the party "dispersed in order to view the rock." Mountford and Strehlow walked together, both trying to take photographs "as the sun got lower and the red colors came out more." Mountford, by his own admission, "became profligate," exposing countless color films to be sure that he "carried home some record of such beauty." He would long treasure these miniature relics and they would continually draw him back to the rock.

Like the photographs McKinnon had taken during his visit in 1932, Mountford's photographs and Strehlow's film (*Board of Inquiry*)—the first-ever moving image of Uluru—were some of the

Shadow of camel,
Strehlow, and
Mountford, 1935

earliest examples of tourist consumption of the rock. Created in the very same moment Yokununna's body was exhumed, they were carried back to Alice Springs together with his remains—the frontier's cadaverous legacy and the romance of the rock riding cheek by jowl in the same camel boxes.

By the time Strehlow and Mountford had returned to their camp at Maggie Springs, it was dark. The party left at midday the following day, their "camel string winding its way back to civilization through the rank grass and bloodwood trees." As they moved farther, "the rock getting smaller and fainter in the distance," Mountford kept turning back to gaze at it one last time. He was already determined that he would return to "explore its numberless caves . . . walk around its base, and look up its mighty red walls."

When they were reunited with the others at Angas Downs Station, they told them their stories of the rock and how it had captured their imaginations. As John Sexton later explained to the press: "The members of the party who visited Ayers Rock and saw its numerous caves, paintings, and rock holes, with Mount Olga in the distance, standing like an ancient city, with domes and towers, will be able to depict first-hand a portion of the interior which has been described by explorers as an artist's wonderland. Beside its arresting natural features, it is a sacred sanctuary, where the Aborigines have gathered for generations for their ceremonials."

Mountford and Strehlow had glimpsed with their own eyes what the Reverend Ernest Kramer had sensed before them: Uluru's sacrosanct status for the Anangu. In 1928, Kramer held a Christian service south of Uluru, describing the rock as "the most sacred spot in all [the] country around where natives come for their ceremonies." But in 1935, they did not see the Anangu. Baldwin Spencer, in 1894, had observed their "whirlies," detailed their method for cooking kangaroo, and marveled at their collection of the honey ant. Unintentionally surprising one of their camps, he narrowly escaped being

Northeast side of Ayers Rock, 1935

speared. By the mid-1930s, nearly all of the Anangu—for whom Uluru had always been a regular campsite and sacred place—had departed, many living farther west in the Petermann Ranges Reserve. Mountford and Strehlow had arrived at a rare moment in the rock's fifty-thousand-year history of human occupation: its traditional owners were largely absent.

On June 16, as they approached Hermannsburg, Strehlow was keen to enjoy one more night of peace amid the "great hush of eternity." He could already feel "civilization . . . with all its unquiet, purposeless turmoil," looming ahead of them. That night, the party shared the last of "a plum pudding" to celebrate McKinnon's thirty-third birthday. The superficial bonhomie disguised Strehlow's and Mountford's true feelings about the inquiry—their concerns regarding Cleland's impartiality and McKinnon's attempts to tailor the evidence to his advantage. To them, the chances of the board finding their traveling companion guilty already appeared slim. Immediately after the exhumation, Mountford had noticed that Cleland seemed uninterested in taking more evidence, even when White's line of questioning appeared to have McKinnon cornered.

When they reached Alice Springs on June 23, "after a long [three-week] journey of 915 miles by truck and camels," Strehlow knew that much of the evidence the board had collected was little more than "lies and subterfuge." He vividly described one final "dramatic moment" that took place in a "bleak tin shed" at Alice Springs: "Numberlin alleged that McKinnon had come to his cell before the arrival of the Board, and persuaded him to give false evidence—to tell the Board that McKinnon had never hit him, and had always been kind to him etc." Wherever it seemed necessary, McKinnon relied on coercion, either to extract the evidence he sought from Aboriginal witnesses or to cover his tracks.

In the last week of June, McKinnon and his trackers attended the board's private sessions in Alice Springs before heading back to

Board of inquiry hearing evidence at Coolata Springs, 1935; McKinnon standing at left

Charlotte Waters. Years later, he "gleefully" recalled Carbine's contempt for the proceedings—he'd spat on the floor repeatedly until he was told to stop. Once the investigations were over, John Cleland took the train back to Adelaide, arriving there on the evening of June 27, 1935. Cleland, who had long been obsessed with the prospect of Aboriginal extinction, believed that it was Australians' "bounden duty to see that the natives who have been dispossessed of their territory and the homes of their ancestors should be dealt with as gently and sympathetically as possible." "If it is their fate to pass out of existence," he told an audience in Adelaide after his return, "let us feel that we have done our best to delay that fateful day." Over the next six weeks, together with Sexton and White, he wrote the board's report.

On the same train returning to Adelaide with Cleland was Cecil Madigan, who had been scouring the country for geological samples and had collected hundreds of "fossils and rock specimens." Madigan, of course, knew all the members of the board and was close to McKinnon. Even before the long train journey back to Adelaide, he had formed a view regarding the inquiry's findings. On June 24, still in Alice Springs, he told a journalist he was confident that "the general local opinion is that the findings of the Board can only be noncommittal." That local opinion was not drawn from a very large sample. Cleland had no doubt spoken with Madigan about the report that was still to be written, quietly reassuring him that McKinnon would not be found guilty.

The board of inquiry's findings were published in early September 1935. The report itself was not released in its entirety—the government claimed there was no precedent or need to do so. Hundreds of pages long, the report contained as many claims for adequate compensation for damage to motor vehicles as detailed examinations of the shooting at Ayers Rock one year earlier. It was immediately clear that Cleland, Sexton, and White had struggled to reach a unanimous

decision. First, there were no witnesses to the shooting of Yokununna, either by McKinnon or by Carbine. As the board worked its
way through the sequence of events, it found much of McKinnon's
evidence difficult to believe. Yokununna, who could not speak English, was clearly "ignorant" of the charges laid against him. All three
members condemned the system which allowed for "the pursuit or
arrest of Aboriginals by armed Aboriginal trackers who have no
knowledge of the pursued prisoners, or suspects' language," although,
in this case, Carbine could indeed speak Yokununna's language.

They also had grave "ethical objections" to the shooting. "McKinnon," they observed, "stated that . . . without taking any aim whatever, [he] presented his pistol and fired into the cave, but did not
expect to hit Yokununna." "Although he could not speak Yokununna's language (Luritja), he had called him repeatedly by voicing [his]
name in English in tones of command and entreaty." McKinnon's
life was never in "actual danger." They could not "bring themselves
to believe that his second shot was fired under circumstances where
the direction of the bullet could not be calculated with the deliberate
intention of seriously wounding the fugitive." "It would have been far
better," they resolved, "to have let Yokununna escape entirely, rather
than effect his capture by use of firearms." McKinnon had "acted too
hastily." "The shooting, ethically, was not justified." They speculated
on his mental state at the time, doubting his claim that after such an
arduous journey he had remained "calm and collected."

Yet despite all their suspicions and doubts, they were torn.

"From a legal point of view, no charge could be maintained in a
court of law against . . . McKinnon, who, in the exercise of his duty
as a member of the constabulary, took measures to prevent the further escape of the prisoner." At times, they appeared to contradict
their own reasoning, arguing on the one hand that McKinnon's actions were justified under the law, at the same time as they argued

that he should have ignored his legal right to "arrest [Yokununna] . . . with firearms if necessary" and instead allowed him to escape. The whole saga, they concluded forlornly, was a "tragedy on the lower slopes of this vast rock situated in the heart of Central Australia." The public release of the findings only seemed to reinforce the board's labored equivocation. They stated:

1. That the evidence tendered to the Inquiry does not show that those mentioned were guilty of any ill-treatment of Aborigines, with the exception of the thrashing of natives at Hermannsburg by Constable McKinnon which was undertaken at the request of a responsible officer of the Mission (Mr. Mattner).
2. That in view of the evidence obtained by the Board of Inquiry we are of the opinion that the shooting of Yokununna by Constable McKinnon at Ayers Rock, though legally justified, was not warranted.

McKinnon recorded the result in his logbook, albeit selectively: "Finding of Board of Inquiry: Shooting of Yokununna legally justified. Proved guilty of thrashing two Aboriginals at Hermannsburg at request of responsible Mission official." The words "at request of" suggested he was merely following instructions, when in fact he was not bound to do so. Reluctant to acknowledge the board's full findings and commit them to his personal record, he failed to mention that the board had also found that his shooting of Yokununna was "not warranted." Underneath his entry, he drew two thick lines, as if this was the end of the matter.

Newspapers across the continent carried short articles with the news of McKinnon's exoneration: BLACKS IN NORTH. ALLEGED ILL-TREATMENT. STATEMENTS REFUTED; REPRIMAND ONLY. Journalists made much of the board's extraordinary travels—"700 miles by motor car and motor truck, and 240 miles by camels"—and the lengths its members went to in order to procure evidence: "Twenty natives and 26 Europeans were examined, and 33 natives were interviewed." The language echoed the board's triumphant perception of its ability to conquer the vast spaces of the Territory: "The area where the incidents occurred . . . [was] approximately 15,000 square miles with a resident white population of under 30." McKinnon was not to be dismissed—that would be "too severe a penalty"—merely reprimanded for showing "excessive zeal." His shooting of Yokununna was an "error of judgment." The same reports stressed his "excellent record"—a police officer who was "highly thought of by the department and by the Minister of the Interior, who met him during a recent tour of Central Australia." Even in a country as vast as Australia, in which the national capital was thousands of miles from the center of the continent, it was still possible for a policeman like McKinnon to be known personally by his federal minister.

The report of the board's conclusions sounded all too familiar. What the public could not see were the private reflections of Strehlow and Mountford, who both saw the board's findings as a whitewash, or Sexton's dissenting letter, written on July 8, 1935, which he appended to the board's report. There was so much evidence submitted of a "contradictory nature," Sexton argued, that it was "well-nigh impossible to ascertain the real truth." Besides, he explained, "the natives were too afraid to give true evidence on any matters affecting the police. . . . It was openly stated that it would be impossible to live in the outback unless a fear complex could be created in the native mind." As ever, police violence was as much about spreading psychological terror as establishing the settlers' superiority. As for McKinnon, Sexton had little time for his version of events.

> Constable McKinnon stoutly denied that he had thrashed
> the boys [at Hermannsburg] and it was only when Mr.

Mattner, the relieving officer, gave evidence that the truth was revealed. Mr. Mattner told the Board that he had asked Constable McKinnon to thrash the boys and that he had carried out his request. The denial by Constable McKinnon of flogging the boys shows his utter lack of veracity and in my judgment most seriously discounts any evidence tendered by him to the Board of Inquiry. . . . [McKinnon's claim that he was hit on the finger by a stone thrown by Yokununna is nothing more than a] concoction introduced into the narrative in order to justify the use of firearms. . . . It is not credible that a poor, wounded fugitive hotly pursued, shot at and wounded by the tracker, would have either energy or strength left to put up any kind of defense against his powerful adversaries. . . . [McKinnon] had not the chivalry to give Yokununna a sporting chance of escape which any fair minded man would have done under the circumstances. . . . [He] should have exercised discipline over his spirit, [and] preserved his mental balance and poise . . . instead of resorting to arms. . . . [He] was at no time in any personal danger. . . . I am of the opinion that Constable McKinnon should be impeached for this crime but I am well aware that with the relations existing in the North between the white and black race that no jury composed of white men would bring in a verdict against him. Under these circumstances I consider that the authorities should mark their displeasure of his deed by dismissing him from the service of the government. This I realize would in no way be commensurate for the wrong done but it would at least act as a deterrent to others who might be disposed to hold cheaply the lives of the King's subjects in the outback country.

Sexton had spelled out in detail what Strehlow and Mountford had suspected all along. McKinnon was not telling the whole truth. He had concealed crucial facts from the moment he gave evidence to the inquest into Kai-Umen's death, when he stated that Yokununna "died as a result of a bullet that was fired," failing to explain the full circumstances. Given the Commonwealth's response to the report, it clearly had similar suspicions. Although Lyons accepted the board's findings, and the inquiry's report was certainly a marked improvement on the official response to the Coniston Massacre in 1928, his government's refusal to make the report public smacked of a cover-up. It protected McKinnon. It denied the public the opportunity to read Sexton's letter and the damning Aboriginal testimony regarding McKinnon's behavior, and it shielded federal and Territory authorities from the wave of public protest that would surely have followed.

Even then, the government could not escape criticism, with church and humanitarian groups denouncing the board's findings. Privately, the Lyons government made it clear that McKinnon had "exceeded his authority," instructing the Territory administration that in the future, police had "no authority to inflict corporal punishment" and that "shooting should be obviated as far as possible." While many of the reforms to policing in the Territory recommended by the board—uniformed native police, banning the possession of firearms by trackers, refraining from laying charges in matters of "tribal law" or "where no white man is involved," and "rigorously" pursuing white-on-black assaults—would either be ignored or take years to implement, a handful of measures were adopted immediately. To ensure that police were more accountable in the Territory, the government decided to appoint a patrol officer, someone who would act as a culturally informed, ethical overseer, patrolling the backcountry southwest of Alice Springs, administering corporal punishment ("a reasonable whipping . . . after consultation with the old men of the tribe") in preference to jail terms. The first to be appointed, in 1936, without the power to administer such whippings, was none other than Strehlow, who would serve for the next six years as "the first full-time Commonwealth public servant dedicated to Aboriginal affairs."

In later life, whenever McKinnon spoke of the events at Uluru in late 1934, he made sure to read from the statement he submitted to the board of inquiry—"Story of the Escape of Six Prisoners." He never allowed the public record of his story to vary. On a small number of occasions, he permitted himself an addendum, if only to further justify his actions: the only "adverse finding" of the board, he claimed, was "that I had thrashed two young persistent, petty thieves . . . at the request of [the superintendent of Hermannsburg Mission]." "The members of the Board, though most thorough in their investigations, were kind to me and were as considerate as they could be at all times. While traveling around the country I put myself on as the cook of the party."

Interviewed formally in the 1980s and 1990s by separate oral history units in the Northern Territory, he continually stressed the settlers' good intentions—"people can say what they like," he stated defiantly, "the police [and station people] were good to the blacks. . . . [They] *generally* had fair treatment." Before speaking of the Coniston Massacre, he paused and asked: "Am I allowed to recall this?" Yet even after he admitted that so many more Aboriginal people were killed than official accounts suggested ("over eighty"), he stood behind the findings of the Coniston board of inquiry: "At the end of it," he stressed, "it was found that it was all justified. Nobody committed any offenses." His words resounded.

The two government boards of inquiry had now allowed police to claim that their actions had been vindicated. "Nobody committed any offenses." Not Constable William George Murray in 1928. Not Constable Bill McKinnon in 1934. Yet, as one reporter noted after the 1935 board of inquiry's findings were announced, there was "something radically wrong" in central Australia. Between 1928 and 1935, five policemen, one-eighth of the Territory's entire force, including Murray and McKinnon, had been suspended from duty while trials or inquiries into their alleged cruelty toward Aboriginal people were conducted. All were acquitted and all continued in their jobs. The only consequence for McKinnon for his indiscretions at Uluru was that he had to wait twelve months for his annual salary increment.

The inside of Barrow Creek Telegraph Station in 2013, with shooting hole at right

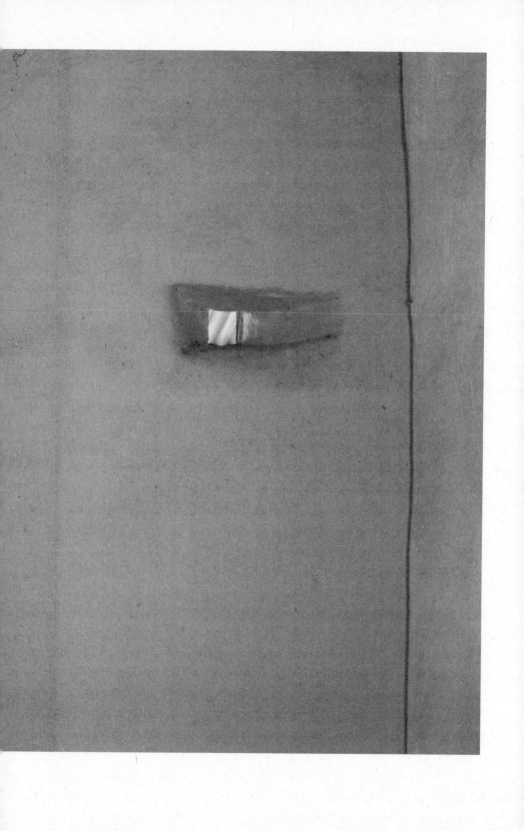

6

ROUND TRIPS

n February 1936, after learning of the board's findings, McKinnon and Doreen finally set off on a delayed honeymoon trip—a "4,000 mile circuitous motor tour." They drove their 1923 Dodge 4 Tourer from Alice Springs through northwestern Queensland to Nambour, where they stayed with McKinnon's father, and then south to Mullumbimby, where they spent three weeks with his brother, James. It was his first holiday since arriving in Alice Springs in 1931, and as on every other journey he'd made in central Australia, he kept a daily log of his progress across the country. "Called at Chalmer's Macdonald Downs and had morning tea . . . arrived at Kidman's 'Huckitta' Station and had dinner with Harry Brumby. He showed us a door of the homestead with seven spear holes in it. These were made 11 years ago during an attack by the natives on the manager W. Madrill." Most of his journal entries complained about bad roads, "sandy wastes," punctured tires, and the daily ordeal of being "tortured by flies and heat."

At one point, near the Queensland border, they were towed out of the river by Constable William Murray, who was stationed nearby. Like McKinnon's camel patrols through the interior, this marathon honeymoon road trip made lighthearted news in northern New South Wales: "They will journey via Sydney, Melbourne, Adelaide and Oodnadatta back to Alice Springs, thus completing the round trip. They are accompanied by their mascot, Pete, a wire-haired fox-terrier." Once the inquiry's findings were handed down, McKinnon's image in the press returned to its previous incarnation—a figure of mystique, the center's wiry, knockabout storyteller in uniform—if it had ever really been challenged. In the weeks and months he spent driving across the country with Doreen, did their conversation ever turn to the events at Uluru in late 1934? Or the allegations of mistreatment? Were they referred to obliquely, brushed off in an aside, or silenced entirely within him?

For the next few years, while he continued his camel patrols and relieved at isolated police stations throughout the Northern Territory, Doreen accompanied him. Anxious for her safety while he was away, he arranged for a tracker "to camp on the verandah overnight to protect her." Many years later, he described their roving lifestyle as "a hard and unfair life" for his wife. "I was often away," he admitted, "and [Doreen] would be alone with no white people for 70 miles. But we had our happy times too."

Between 1935 and 1941, McKinnon and Doreen moved from one police station to the next. Some, like Charlotte Waters (which he officially closed in 1938) and Barrow Creek, were former Overland Telegraph stations, "top quality brick buildings" as McKinnon described them, where he could still see "the holes in the walls" that the station workers had used to "defend themselves against Aboriginal raids."

The introduction of "pedal wireless sets" was a "godsend," enabling him to communicate much quicker than before. Doreen's job—compulsory for police wives at stations such as these—was to take the weather records "every three hours during the day," between

6 a.m. and 9 p.m., for which she received "about a shilling a day." McKinnon's tasks were varied: everything from "servicing the cattle station people" to handing out weekly rations to Aboriginal people on Fridays, and rescuing (and occasionally burying) white men and women who had ventured into the center without sufficient water and food, nearly all of them driven mad "through privation and thirst."

In late 1941, just before moving north to Darwin, they left the new police station at Finke Siding, where they were credited with starting "one of the best gardens in the Territory." The Aboriginal people to whom McKinnon had been handing out rations every Friday put on a farewell corroboree for them, just as had happened three years earlier at Charlotte Waters. But newspaper articles on his exploits in the "trackless wastes of the interior" continued to betray his true attitudes to Aboriginal people he suspected of having committed "crimes."

In 1939, reflecting on his role in the Territory, he described "the Northern Territory Aboriginal" as "a cunning fellow [who] will, until eventually cornered in interrogation and cross-examination, pile lies upon lies." "If he thinks," said McKinnon, "that you know who committed the offense he will confess to the deed or give a true statement through an interpreter." Precisely what methods he used to "corner" the accused he did not say. Journalists, however, continued to present him as the victim of Aboriginal attacks, a policeman who was "obliged" on several occasions to "fight for his life."

During the years after the inquiry, when he corresponded with his family he often reflected on the ordeals of his peripatetic life. In September 1938, he wrote to his sister from Finke Siding, describing the frustrations of his job. The new police station that was supposed to have been finished in time for his posting had taken longer than expected to complete. As a result, he and Doreen were forced to stay in temporary accommodation in Alice Springs, living in "four different houses in the town" while he continued his patrols. When they finally moved into the new station, life there was still trying.

Dear Bella,

At last you will get your long overdue letter. I have written no private letters for months, as it has been just about impossible to settle down to it. . . . Finke Railway Siding is 40 miles northwest from Charlotte Waters. . . . [Last month, I] went to Charlotte on my own, returned with a load of iron, some beef from a drover, and two old crippled lubras [Aboriginal women]. Had two punctures then a blowout so decided to come home on a flat tire as it was past redemption & my spare tire was at Horseshoe Bend . . . three miles from home the rim was pulled off and destroyed. Lit a fire for the lubras—it was night time then, and walked home. . . . Wired south for two new tires to arrive on train . . . [but] the blasted tires did not come so we are again held up. . . . All this is typical of my disturbed existence over a period of many months. Even the dogs cause [me trouble]. I bashed Pete's brains out with a tire lever for killing a crate of fowls that we had just taken off the train. . . . Then, our other dog, "Red," a lovely dog, caught a new disease that is going around . . . and I had to shoot him a week ago. I then cremated him. . . . All these experiences will help you to understand why I am not the correspondent I used to be. Perhaps when we get properly settled here I will make a good comeback. . . . I am also ordering a new typewriter by this mail, on time payment. It is a necessity as all my correspondence, returns etc. are done in duplicate or triplicate. It will last me till I am 60, when I will probably give it to my kids. . . . Our home is not yet fenced in, but will be in the near future. When it is I will start a flower garden & lawns in front, & vegetable garden & fowl run out the back. . . . Things are very dry here, a good rain would do the world of good. . . . We had a dance here [on the verandah] last Saturday week. The fettlers, the pump [man] and his wife, two station men and the wife of one . . . one of the fettlers played his accordion. Everybody had a good time and they all went home at midnight. . . . I took part in conveying Lady Dugan (S.A. Governor's wife) & her party around the country. She sent me a beautiful note wallet, mounted and inscribed "W. McK." Have not written to thank her. I probably will not now as I have left it too long. In any case, I will not see her anymore. . . .

Love to all and best wishes to you both, Bill.

The following year, he wrote to his brother, James, describing his journey to Adelaide for the birth of his daughter, Susan. Doreen had gone into hospital at the same time as her mother, who was gravely ill. Writing "man to man," McKinnon explained his feelings to "Jimmie."

"Susan Mary" was born at 9 the same night [he arrived]. She only weighed 6 lbs. 13 oz., but has been putting on weight ever since. She only appeared half the size that I had expected to see. Dord had a fairly good time through it, and when I visited her 20 minutes after she was all smiles and said "There she is." She is breast feeding it and looks like continuing. Can you picture me visiting three women daily at the hospital for a fortnight? It was a real morbid experience for me, I told them I would be much happier if it was a pub instead of a hospital. . . . [Dord's mother] used to tell me every

McKinnon with his daughter, Susan, circa 1941

day that she would not see the night out, but unfortunately
she is not a woman of her word. . . . I got real fed up in
Adelaide with nothing in particular to do, so finally wired up
for permission to resume duty still another week early.

Despite its hardships, McKinnon longed to be out in the center on patrol, where he would "often call at a station where the white man in charge had not seen another white man for weeks and I might not have seen one either." "We would sit all night talking," he recalled fondly, "and boil the billy every few hours." This camaraderie—the unspoken bonds shared by a small group of lonely white males—appears to have been one of the deepest emotional experiences of his life. He would hark back to it decades later.

In 1941, shortly before he moved from Finke Siding to Tennant Creek, he wrote to Bella about his most recent patrol, having brought in "three blacks" to Alice Springs for thieving. He'd gone ahead to Alice with his "prisoners," he told her, and had asked his trackers to bring the camels back to town, but soon discovered they'd "dawdled on the way home." "They had over 20 blacks and their dogs with them," he wrote. "They had the camels all separated and carrying the tribes' gear. They were still not home with my camp gear by the time I was ready for another trip, so I had to waste two days in the car looking for them. I found them with all my rations finished and everything in a filthy condition. I naturally started off by giving the two trackers a good walloping, then shot all the dogs and ordered the mob back to Alice Springs where they came from." In the same letter, he described how, in another assignment, at Mount Cavanagh Station, he'd exhumed yet another body of an Aboriginal man and presented the evidence in court.

My two murderers have been committed for trial.
Although there is strong evidence against them I will not be

surprised if they get out of it as Territory juries seldom convict a white man of an offense against blacks. These two should go along as they used a particularly brutal method. They bashed their victim with a heavy rifle and a pistol, kicked him, then put one end of a length of fencing wire around his neck, tied the other end to the back of a truck and dragged him along for some distance. I took his head in as an exhibit. It ponged [smelled] a bit.

McKinnon lived by the Territory's unwritten laws as much as he did by its ever-changing ordinances and regulations. Although he was clearly offended by the manner in which these two white men had killed their victim, he had relied on brute force himself when he wanted to extract confessions from Aboriginal men or was desperate to track them down. On this occasion, he presented his gruesome evidence as he had done so many times before, but the court acquitted the two men (Herbert Kitto and Patrick Deconlay) because the head "could not be identified conclusively as that of the alleged victim." For Olive Pink, who sat watching the proceedings in Alice Springs, the decision was an indictment of British justice. While Aboriginal people were all too readily imprisoned for assault or murder, Europeans were rarely convicted of violence against Aboriginal people.

Violence was embedded in everyday life—both Indigenous and non-Indigenous—on the central Australian frontier. Carefully prescribed in certain circumstances, such as payback, contravention of sacred law, or capital punishment, it was also practiced by Aboriginal men resisting the invasion of their lands, by police enforcing the law, and by countless lawless individuals imposing their own brand of "rough justice" in order to exert their authority and seize the country for themselves. Lawfully or unlawfully, it was the means by which much conflict and errant behavior was resolved and punished—a language spoken, if not equally administered or understood, by all.

In October 1941, McKinnon and Doreen moved north to Darwin. By the end of the year, together with young Susan, Doreen was evacuated weeks before two Japanese bombing raids killed 235 people in February 1942. McKinnon fled his room at the police barracks only "seconds" before it was "blown out of existence." Two days later, he "dug" his camera "out of the wreckage" to photograph the devastation. He spent the remainder of the year and the next stationed at Borroloola, on the McArthur River, thirty miles upstream from the Gulf of Carpentaria, before he was reunited with his family at Tennant Creek in 1944.

While he was at Borroloola, Numberlin, "prisoner number 574," and Nangee, "prisoner number 580," were released after serving more than eight years of their ten-year sentence in Alice Springs jail for the "murder" of Kai-Umen. The two men survived the time they'd spent in prison despite a number of stabbings by fellow inmates. On one occasion Numberlin was accused of having in his cell "one pack of playing cards and one vegetable knife, Contrary to Section 34 of the Prison Act 1869–70," for which he was found guilty and lost one month of his remission. On another, he was charged with "abusive language, acting in a defiant and aggressive manner and disobeying the order [of the prison guard] to wear his boots," and sentenced to a week of solitary confinement with meager rations of bread and water. On the day of their release, the men were each issued a pair of trousers, a shirt, and a pair of boots, and left to make their way back home. It is not known if they ever arrived. Once outside the prison walls, they walked out of history.

McKinnon might have felt that justice had been done, but the recollections of one of his colleagues suggest his patience with the law's due process sometimes wore thin. One of his juniors at Tennant

Creek, Bob Darken, claimed in his memoir that McKinnon had told him he was "a silly bugger" for not killing an Aboriginal man who had attacked a missionary's wife, Mrs. Long, with a boomerang. Darken also recalled Police Paddy telling him "once about the time he was Bill McKinnon's tracker and Bill shot a few blacks in a cave in the Petermann Ranges." Paddy explained to Darken that "McKinnon didn't shoot all of them." "I shot two," Paddy told him straight-faced.

In January 1946, four months after the war ended, McKinnon and Doreen returned to Darwin, moving into a house that still "had bomb holes through the roof and the ceilings." Later that year, McKinnon was again charged with mistreating an Aboriginal prisoner. Arresting the man late one night, he was completely unaware that he was being watched by C. K. Ward, Darwin's stipendiary magistrate. Looking through his kitchen window, Ward saw two police officers pull up in a truck. "Both then heaved the native over the back of the truck . . . in such a way that he would land in the truck head down, and in fact I saw his legs above the tailboard of the truck." As the truck drove off, Ward walked around to the back of his home and stood on the landing as it passed by, "illuminated for a few seconds by a streetlight." "I distinctly saw the forearm of a white man moving as though delivering three or four punches at some object sitting or lying in the back of the truck," he stated. "As the truck passed us I heard whimpering and crying coming from the vehicle. There is no doubt in my mind that the native was most brutally handled by the policemen and savagely assaulted by one of them. I was unable to see who the policemen were, but I recognized the truck and the uniforms. I have been informed since that the native was handcuffed."

As a result of an internal police inquiry, the prisoner, Leo, gave evidence that the "bloke with the mustache, a sergeant," had pushed his head down—he showed the bump on his head—"punched" him and held him "down on the floor of the truck by the neck." Then he threatened to "knock [him] down with [his] baton" if he made trouble. Pulling a revolver on him, he shouted: "If you run away I'll show you something." McKinnon was officially charged by the administrator on August 17, 1946, for abusing and beating Leo. In his formal response to the administrator two weeks later, he was characteristically defiant: "I deny the truth of the charge . . . One of the native's main idiosyncrasies when under the influence of liquor is to yell and cry, and this is one of the chief causes of Mr. Ward's delusion that he was being dealt with in a brutal manner." On September 6, Arthur Driver, administrator of the Northern Territory, informed McKinnon of the result of the inquiry: "I completely exonerate you from the charge."

In 1951, McKinnon reached the top ranks of the Northern Territory Police when he was promoted to senior inspector. In 1955, he was passed over as superintendent. McKinnon believed this was because of his strict policing of betting laws in Darwin, and that a businessman and bookmaker had pressed his superiors to move him on. He and his family would remain in Darwin—a place he loathed—until 1955. Later that year, he was stationed back at Alice Springs, which had been transformed by its pivotal role during the war. By now, the "protection" policies that he had enforced vigorously since his arrival in 1931 had been replaced by the equally insidious policy of assimilation. McKinnon's house was next to the courthouse, which was frequented by none other than the indefatigable Olive Pink.

There was no love lost between them. She saw him as "unclean," a man who should have been convicted of Yokununna's murder twenty years earlier. He saw her as a "regular nuisance," a person with a "most dangerous tongue" who constituted "a menace to the security of Court House business." They argued in public, over McKinnon's back fence, and at the police station, especially after McKinnon banned her daily visits to inquire about upcoming cases involving Aboriginal defendants. Pink—who was evicted from her rented hut on Gregory Terrace and regularly harassed by the town's officials, who disliked her outspokenness and eccentric manner—was in no doubt that her lifelong determination to call out the injustices done to Aboriginal people had cost her dearly. Racism in Alice was deeply ingrained. On the streets, the legacy of the frontier was still visible. In the 1950s—the last decade of McKinnon's active service—no lesser authority than the Alice Springs Country Women's Association remarked that it was still possible to see "white men in Central Australia today walking on spear-scarred legs."

In December 1959, together with five other Northern Territory policemen, McKinnon was awarded a medal by the queen for long service and good conduct. He finally retired in 1962. When his last day in the force arrived, his acting superintendent described McKinnon admiringly as a "strict disciplinarian" who had proved that he could "handle men." Station owners praised him as a "sterling friend" who "played the game over the years, and . . . carried out his duties with justice and tact." McKinnon's retirement was covered in the local press, which eulogized him as "one of the originals," noting that at the official ceremony, he was presented with a "canteen of cutlery and a wallet of notes" to mark his years of service.

In retirement, and having had a six-thousand-pound New South Wales lottery win in 1957 (around US$150,000 in 2021), McKinnon and Doreen moved to Buderim in Queensland. There, he busied himself tending his archive and writing up his recollections, especially of his first three years in the Territory police: "I have always looked on my first three years on full-time camel patrol," he remarked, "as the most satisfying and most useful period of my whole service . . . The country was full of interest." As he entered his last decades, this tiny cluster of distant years became the most brightly lit period of his life. Every memory tracked back to his first patrols southward from Alice Springs—makeshift camps under the stars, months on end of hardship and heroic improvisation, "native criminals" mercilessly hunted down, victims' bodies exhumed and decapitated, and the unforgettable feeling of freedom as his trackers, Paddy and Carbine, led him through a seemingly endless expanse of fenceless country.

Such was the bloodstained romance of Constable Bill McKinnon, the center's law enforcer. He filed his best photographs away, including ones of Uluru and the Olgas. He was fond of reminding friends, and the procession of journalists and local historians who came to hear his story, that he was the first white man to climb the Olgas. He wanted to be remembered as "Mac," the roving policeman who spun "a good yarn of the old Australian outback"—a man who would "never die" in popular memory.

In early September 1936, Ted Strehlow returned to Uluru with Bertha James, a brilliant classics student with whom he'd fallen in love three years earlier at Adelaide University. They married in December 1935, soon after Strehlow returned from his travels with the board of inquiry. By the time they set out from Hermannsburg with three Aboriginal guides and eleven camels on a fourteen-hundred-mile journey to the Petermann Ranges, Strehlow was combining his linguistic and anthropological research into the Indigenous cultures of central Australia with his new role as Commonwealth patrol officer. Bertha was his soul mate, collaborator, and research assistant.

The couple knew that this trek could take many months. To pass the long hours after dark around the campfire, they read poetry to each other by lamplight. Strehlow's favorite, Bertha recalled fondly, was T. S. Eliot's "The Hollow Men"—"Shape without form, shade without colour / Paralysed force, gesture without motion"—the poem's title, among other things, evoking the morally bankrupt Europeans in Joseph Conrad's *Heart of Darkness*. It was a hollowness that Strehlow had seen in the faces of many of the white men he'd encountered in the center.

Six weeks in, Bertha told Strehlow she was pregnant. Suffering from morning sickness, she struggled in the unforgiving terrain. In late August, at Pitaldi, in the Petermann Ranges, she miscarried. Over the next few weeks, there were times when Strehlow feared for her life. Leaving Pitaldi and traveling for about "sixty miles," they approached Mount Olga, which Bertha described longingly as a "blue shadow on the horizon" with "many domes." As she came closer, she watched in amazement as its color changed to "rose pink and then to dark red," its "rocky mass" forming a "cluster of gigantic boulders heaped together." Carried like a wounded soldier "on the side of a camel in the stretcher-frame" Strehlow had made for her, Bertha felt her condition improve when a group of Aboriginal women gave her a medicinal herb, which she took as a tea infusion.

Two miles from the rock, Strehlow described the "poetry" of the landscape that surrounded them: "lovely mulga thickets, bloodwood watercourses, snowy mulga grass [and] sweet flowering white acacia blossoms." On reaching Mutitjulu Waterhole, Bertha had time to recover. "We found a quantity of water on the southern side of the rock," she wrote, "and replenished our supplies at a pool which was icy cold because the sun's rays could not reach over the high rock wall [of Uluru]."

For Strehlow, the memory of McKinnon's shooting of Yokununna and the inquiry's retrieval of his remains was still fresh in his mind. Writing in his journal as Bertha recovered, he struggled to reconcile the rock as a place of "peace and undisturbed serene beauty" with the "cruelty and viciousness" he knew it had witnessed. For whitefella pilgrims like Strehlow, the stories from the Anangu Dreaming that were etched onto the cave walls near Mutitjulu Waterhole, and which he tried in vain to comprehend, would continue to be trailed by stories of violence.

Between 1940 and 1960, Charles Mountford returned five times to Mutitjulu Waterhole to study the rock art that had so transfixed him by lamplight in 1935. Yet even after decades of study, he was forced to admit that "without the explanation of the artist who produced them," he could do little more than guess their true meaning. His impressions of the rock—"there seems to be nothing to which Ayers Rock can be likened"—remained equally constricted. Undeterred, he never lost his romantic association with the place, writing articles, publishing several books (in which he managed to get many details of Anangu culture spectacularly wrong), and accompanying a large group of students from Sydney's Knox Grammar School on a much-publicized trek led by Alice Springs resident and tour guide Len Tuit in 1950, when he was dismayed to discover that visitors had scrawled their names over some of the paintings he'd photographed years earlier.

Similar reports of vandalism could be found well into the 1970s, when tour leaders reportedly threw buckets of water over paintings in order to "bring out the colors" for their clients' souvenir photographs. Meanwhile, other visitors washed in the spring with soap and shampoo, polluting the water hole.

Drawn back repeatedly to the rock, Mountford heard stories about what had happened when McKinnon shot Yokununna in 1934. On one occasion, in the 1940s, he was told by "Kinkiba," a relative of Yokununna: "Yokununna bin tell other blackfella . . . me close-up bin finish. You fella hide in *bulba* (cave) and when policemen bin kill me, you go 'long to Kata Tjuta (Mt Olga)." It was the first of several damning Indigenous accounts of the shooting that would appear over the coming decades, all of which, although they varied in emphasis and detail, left little doubt about the truth of the matter. When Mountford contemplated the possibility that Yokununna had sacrificed his life so that his friends could flee, he thought it an act of heroism "which, in a civilized community, would have been commemorated in verse and song and become part of a people's heritage." Before he died in 1976, he requested that his ashes be scattered in the same cave where he'd sat silent and motionless in 1935.

Mountford's journeys to the rock demonstrate that more than any other place in the country, Uluru was becoming a barometer of Australia's rapidly shifting understanding of Aboriginal Australia. The change was swift and remarkable. In 1937, after a young schoolteacher from New South Wales set out from Alice Springs for Uluru on his motorbike and was later found dead, Cecil Madigan warned his readers that traveling to Ayers Rock was a "safe trip only for camels." Although the Australian National Travel Association had already rendered Uluru a "sacred pilgrimage center" from the 1930s, there were relatively few visitors until numbers started to rise steeply from four thousand per year in the early 1960s—when plans to build a cable car to the top of the rock were considered but not developed—to thirty thousand little more than a decade later.

By the 1950s, Uluru's relative isolation from Australia's largest centers of population was already shattered. The arrows of penetration came from all directions: graded dirt roads, airstrips at the foot of the rock, camping grounds, basic facilities, bus tours, and, with them, more and more tourists—lone travelers, school groups, research expeditions, joy flights from Alice Springs, adventure tours, and the *Australian Women's Weekly* "All Women Safari Tour" of 1957—piling their stones dutifully atop the summit, where they used their Kodak cameras to record their conquest. "Picture business," as the Anangu shrewdly called it, was suddenly bringing whitefellas to their Country in their thousands.

McKinnon, of course, was one of the first to set up shop when he photographed the area in the 1930s. The small Bushells tea jar he left at the top when he climbed the rock in 1932, which came to hold pieces of paper signed by those who reached the summit, could still be found there in the late 1950s. Changes on the summit pointed to the onslaught to come. In 1958, the Division of National Mapping decided to replace the existing pile of stones "with a large stone cairn and trigonometric survey marker with pole and vanes as part of a national mapping program." By 1970, they had erected a "stone pedestal and bronze plaque featuring a directional compass, map of Australia, and an Australian Coat of Arms." Federal authorities were beginning to claim the rock for the nation.

Paddy Uluru returning to Uluru with his family, early 1950s

7

"I AM ULURU"

I n 1950, when the conservationist Arthur Groom described his visit to the rock, he claimed that "most of the natives have deserted its cliffs and caves, and 'moved in' to Ernabella and Hermannsburg Missions." Among those who left the area was Yokununna's brother, Paddy Uluru. He was Uluru's traditional custodian and one of the four men McKinnon had chased to the rock in 1934. When he was interviewed during the inquest into Kai-Umen's death, his first words left no doubt as to his identity: "I belong 'Moolatarra' Tribe, (Uluru) Ayers Rock country." Distressed by what had occurred, Paddy had not returned since the day he fled with the other survivors many years earlier. In the early 1950s, he walked with one camel and his wife and family from their home in exile at Mimili, more than 250 miles southeast, following the songlines from one water hole to the next to his true home. The return to Uluru would prove to be the beginning of the Anangu's journey to reclaim their Country. It was the first time that Paddy's sons, Reggie and Cassidy, had seen Uluru, and they felt frightened by its size. The slightly blurred black-and-white photograph of the family taken not long after their arrival in the early 1950s is cherished by Paddy's descendants today.

One of the first white men Paddy met at Uluru was Bill Harney, a friend of Bill McKinnon and the Ayers Rock–Mount Olga National Park's first ranger and so-called protector of Uluru, a man who would remain ambivalent about the dramatic upsurge in tourism that his own obsessions and publications undoubtedly helped to foster. Reggie recalled Harney's frosty greeting. "He wasn't very welcoming. . . . 'What are you doing here?' he asked. 'This is not your country.' And my father said, 'No, I AM Uluru. This is my country.'"

During the 1960s, many more Anangu, driven away from the stations when the government refused to pay pastoralists for the rations they gave Aboriginal workers, and lured by the prospect of tourism, returned from the surrounding country to live near Uluru. Even so, Paddy's son Cassidy remembered being "kicked out of the tourist area," typical treatment for many of his people, who were perceived by some tour operators as too unseemly a sight for their delicate clients. At one point, around the time the Docker River settlement was established in 1968, 150 miles northwest of Uluru, the operators tried unsuccessfully to persuade the Territory's Welfare Branch to move the Anangu there entirely.

No matter how hard the tour companies tried to push Aboriginal people away from Uluru, their communities dug in. Better roads across the Territory and the availability of cars and welfare money helped the Anangu strengthen traditional networks of communication and establish new ones. As visitor numbers climbed above five thousand per annum, they turned to selling artifacts to tourists, which only increased their dependence on the whitefella economy. They quickly saw that, like Uluru itself, they had become "objects to be photographed" by "trigger-happy" whites—their people spoken to like children and "gaped at" as if they were living exhibits of the "primitive." They chopped firewood for the tourists, washed their clothes, and cleaned their tents. At the same time, they tried to educate them about their culture.

Paddy was dismayed by the tourists' desecration of sacred sites, especially Kulpi Mutitjulu (the Mutitjulu, or "family," Cave), where, as children, he and his brother had painted on the walls. Initially, he fled back to Mimili in disgust, but then he realized it was his responsibility to return to his homeland and protect the rock's sacred sites before they were completely ruined and all cultural knowledge was lost. While feature stories on Uluru and its rock art in the popular press had long described Anangu culture as a "relic" of a bygone age, Paddy was determined to keep his culture alive. Tourists had not only defaced some of the cave's paintings; they'd also graffitied many of its walls. Harney's description of the visitors was damning: "[They speak of the Aborigines] with a candor one would only use at some sale-yard. . . . Many of the tourists are laughing their heads off because the black people ask for a gift in return for allowing the photos of the camels and themselves. Others are trying to get an old man to pull off his shirt so as to get a shot of primitive man. Everyone is wanting to know what the government is doing for these 'wretches.' All are interested in 'blacks.'" The Anangu were depicted as "loiterers" and "itinerants" in their own Country.

Bill Harney slowly gained the trust of Paddy's family and the majority of Anangu, who referred to him affectionately as "everybody's boss." He traveled with them around Uluru and far beyond, "amazed by the wealth of mythology in this country." He was yet another whitefella seeking Indigenous knowledge that he could translate for an audience living thousands of miles away in the major cities and towns. For all his false claims to be *the one* who knew some of the secrets of Anangu culture, Harney knew one or two big things that few other Europeans had apprehended. The "outback," he thought, had become the "inside" of the nation. And it was "the country" itself that was the "living thing . . . the human being is just part of the land." His grappling with Anangu culture had reminded him that Aboriginal people had helped Europeans "freely in the past, yet because of their color and their nomadic way of life, [they] were on the scrapheap in our social structure."

Like Mountford before him, Harney was told the story of Mc-Kinnon's shooting of Yokununna, by "one of the tribesmen" he'd befriended while visiting Angas Downs Station. Harney heard how McKinnon had fired into the cave several times, mortally wounding a defenseless man, who, even after he was dragged mercilessly out of the cave, bravely refused to reveal the whereabouts of Paddy Uluru and the other two escapees. Harney wrote up the story as a parable of the violence and injustice his fellow invaders had meted out to Aboriginal people across the continent. "When the day comes that we understand them as they understand us," he implored, "I hope they will have it in their hearts to forgive us our trespasses against them."

In the last decades of the twentieth century, as scores of scholars, writers, and filmmakers followed in Harney's footsteps to Uluru—among them Robert Layton, Barry Hill, and David Roberts—they were told similar stories of McKinnon's summary execution of Yokununna, many of which had been passed down by Paddy Uluru to members of his family. At every juncture, Uluru's steady emergence as a national symbol and "tourist Mecca," not to mention its sacredness for the Anangu, was entwined with the events near Mutitjulu Waterhole in 1934. No one understood the connection better than Paddy Uluru himself. In 1971, as the Anangu's campaign for land rights was beginning to gather pace, he placed the story of his expulsion almost forty years earlier at the heart of his demands for the return of his land: "Having frightened me," he explained, "[McKinnon] chased me away from there. . . . It is my camp. Uluru is my camp. This is mine, this holy cave; my fathers and grandfathers entrusted me with this cave. . . . Ayers Rock is holy. I am Uluru and these things are mine." The memory of his brother, whose name he rarely if ever mentioned (as required by Anangu law), was the unspoken spur. Paddy knew that Yokununna had sacrificed his life so that he and his compatriots could get away. As the fight for social, economic, and political justice for the Anangu and Aboriginal people across Australia intensified in the 1980s and beyond, the connections between the histories that had collided so dramatically near Mutitjulu Waterhole in 1934 would continue to surface in astonishing ways.

As early as the 1940s, Bill McKinnon's exploits became the stuff of legend, thanks largely to popular authors such as Frank Clune. Clune—always on the lookout for a good story from Australia's "wild west"—first met McKinnon then, and quickly anointed him the "pioneer of the Red Center" and the "conqueror of Ayers Rock." His books mixed travelogue, adventure, and history, and they were written in a racy, dramatic style that proved tremendously popular with readers. Clune's work had helped to create the mystique of the rock—"the giant jewel of the desert . . . home of the ancient spirits of creation"—and he'd long wanted to write up the story of McKinnon's camel patrols in the 1930s. McKinnon seemed eager to assist him, even lending him some logbooks so he could read about his exploits firsthand.

In 1957, Clune sent McKinnon a copy of *The Fortune Hunters*, which he inscribed personally: "To my good friend Bill McKinnon, who told the saga of a camel desert patrol, back in the dark ages." In graphic detail, Clune chronicled the story of McKinnon's hunt for the escaped prisoners in 1934 and the shooting at the rock. The book included photographs taken by McKinnon; one showed him unearthing Kai-Umen's body as his "six prisoners" and trackers Paddy and Carbine stood behind the grave, looking on. Another showed Kai-Umen's skull on a shovel opposite a photo of McKinnon as a young man at Bondi Beach. Determined to paint a heroic portrait—"Well done, Bill McKinnon"—Clune presented McKinnon's version of the story in lurid detail, adding his own embellishments and invented dialogue to create a gripping narrative. Predictably, Aboriginal people appeared as hapless "stone age primitives" compared to the "civilized white [police]man . . . [who] had become a human bloodhound."

In Clune's telling, McKinnon was the fearless, duty-bound law enforcer who would stop at nothing to ensure that justice was done. Determined to apprehend Yokununna, he'd merely "fired a shot at the floor of the cave as a warning." How McKinnon felt when he read the story is difficult to say. He wasn't a writer and he knew that others could tell his story far more effectively than he could. At the same time, he was often annoyed by their factual errors, which he crossed out in the published text, inserting the correct information in pen.

In late 1961, on the eve of McKinnon's retirement, Douglas Lockwood, the Melbourne *Herald*'s correspondent in the Northern Territory, published an article on his thirty-year career in the Territory police force. "Inspector McKinnon," Lockwood claimed, told him "that even after an order from Canberra that [neck] chains must not be used he had to do so to prevent prisoners from escaping." He insisted that "no cruelty or hardship was involved . . . he even demonstrated this by chaining two natives to a tree . . . one with handcuffs and chain and the other with neck collar and chain." For good measure, Lockwood quoted McKinnon at length on the events at Uluru in 1934: "'Near Ayers Rock,' said McKinnon, 'I was forced to shoot [one man] in self-defense when he attacked me. I got back to Alice Springs with 20 prisoners and witnesses on chains.' Inspector McKinnon said he had learned never to be weak with natives. 'Had I been weak my life would often have been in danger.'"

McKinnon was incensed by the article and telegrammed Lockwood immediately to let him know. Lockwood stood his ground, replying the same day. "As far as I'm aware, there is nothing in this that you did not tell me. I have checked it against my notes and find that to be so. I am surprised therefore that you should have thought it a shocking story." McKinnon had a long track record of speaking candidly to journalists only to retract his statements later on.

After he moved to southeast Queensland in 1962, he tried his hand more than once at a memoir. "William McKinnon, 16 September 1968" was a thirty-two-page typed manuscript that mysteriously stopped in mid-sentence at the precise moment his first camel patrol began. Two years later came "Recollections at Random," a much less satisfying, ad hoc collection of anecdotes from his days in the Territory. Aside from occasional newspaper articles recalling his days policing the "sandy wastes" of central Australia, none of his memoirs was published. When interviewed, he lamented the decline of "discipline" in the Territory: "I still cannot help becoming hot under the collar whenever I think of the steady destruction of the natives by Governments in their mistaken ideas of educating and enlightening the poor natives."

When he looked back on his experience in the 1930s, he defended his record at every turn: "It was . . . truly interesting to meet up with camps of uncivilized natives. I never had any trouble with them at all and I used my trackers in establishing good relations and then going round inspecting their wounds, burns etc. I can say I always maintained a 100 percent excellent relationship with natives . . . They were hard times but I knew that I was doing a worthwhile job." When writing about his early police career, he presented himself as a combination of the stern disciplinarian and the Good Samaritan. McKinnon's memory—much like his police logbooks—was an instrument of record and reassurance rather than a means of self-discovery.

He enjoyed recalling finer details, such as the uniform he wore in court in Alice Springs in February 1935: "white tunic and trousers . . .

together with white shoes, socks and helmet." Some photographs of him in his later years showed a man standing to attention wearing the same uniform, as if merely to don the old garb was sufficient to resurrect his earlier self—the policeman who had a "fierce reputation" as a "sharp marksman" and for doing things "by the book." His love of regalia and ritual could also be seen in his lifelong membership in the Masonic Lodge, a secretive, male-only sect popular with police, defense personnel, and many in the legal profession. Regardless of whether the order and authority he sought to exert were clandestine or public, McKinnon's worldview was fiercely conservative.

A frequent correspondent to local and state newspapers in Queensland, he spoke at meetings of the conservative group Young Nationals and local fundraisers. In 1976 he railed against a state teachers' strike: "I would urge the Queensland government to dismiss every teacher in the state who has been foolish enough to allow himself or herself to be led by professional stirrers . . . If they are so dissatisfied with their lot then they would do better to seek some other form of employment, or in some other country." For McKinnon, to resile from one's duty was a form of "disloyalty." The strikers were "law-breakers."

By the time he reached his seventies and eighties, he had become a venerable figure in the folk history of central Australia: the "last of the old bush cops," eulogized as "one of the great police pioneers of the Northern Territory," a man who "doubled as medic, comforter, counselor and mother confessor to many an outback character." He relished the opportunity to tell his stories of policing in the Territory, including his role in the Petrov Affair of 1954, when he was one of several policemen standing on the tarmac as the Constellation plane carrying Evdokia Petrova landed at Darwin Airport. After a brief struggle, he helped disarm the Russian agents escorting her and secure her safety before the plane flew on to Moscow: "Each of the thugs stepped out [from the plane] with his right hand inside the lapel of his coat," he recalled, "a posture which caused me unobtrusively to draw my pistol and prepare for sudden action. I had a perfect target at that stage as I had them lined up against the dawning sky." Newspaper features in the Northern Territory and Queensland described him as "the man who saved Mrs. Petrov." One of his other "milestones" was witnessing the last hangings in the Territory in 1952.

In the late twentieth century, as McKinnon's stature as a legendary figure in Northern Territory history flourished, another history emerged that told a markedly different story of the "early days" in central Australia. The two histories ran parallel, talking *across* rather than *to* each other. Among the Anangu, the story of what had happened to Paddy Uluru and his brother in 1934 was passed from one generation to the next. But aside from a few retellings in publications by Harney, Mountford, and Robert Layton, it remained largely confined to Anangu communities, where McKinnon was remembered for much more than the shooting of Yokununna, as Bob Randall, a member of the Stolen Generations who later ran the health clinic at Mutitjulu, recalled in 2003.

> It must have been about 1937. Bill McKinnon, the policeman who took me [away], was known to our people. He was involved in the murder of an uncle of mine outside a cave at Uluru where he had tried to hide from the pursuing police party. On this occasion, during his routine patrolling of the different stations around Central Australia, he rode into the homestead of Angas Downs, a vast property of spinifex grasses, saltbush and mulga and acacia trees which covers hundreds of square kilometers of Yankunytjatjara traditional land. My people were camped across from the homestead by the banks of the river that was running with water at that time, a rare occurrence.

Because other children had already been stolen by police, my family usually covered my lighter skin with ash from the fire. But on that fateful day I had been swimming. . . . My world, that had once made me feel as big and free as the universe, would now become one which made me feel small and worthless, belonging nowhere. . . . Later, when I was grown up and had managed to track down my family members, I found out from my sister, Junie, that when Constable Bill McKinnon took me away, the mothers began to wail and my Yankunytjatjara grandfather wanted to put a spear through that policeman.

Randall's grandfather wasn't the first (or the last) Indigenous man to think of spearing McKinnon. The potential "payback" (punishment for breaking Aboriginal law) for what happened in 1934, combined with McKinnon's role in enforcing the policy of child removal, had no end date.

McKinnon could not have failed to notice the changes that took place at the rock after he retired. The Anangu's successful fight in the 1970s and 1980s to move from dependent tenants to legally sanctioned owners of their own Country overturned many of the racist assumptions that had guided much of his professional life. After the passage of the Aboriginal Land Rights (Northern Territory) Act 1976—a watershed because it represented the first attempt by the Commonwealth government to give legal recognition to Aboriginal ownership of land—the Anangu moved swiftly to claim what was both morally and legally theirs.

Three years later, in 1979, the recently established Central Land Council lodged a land claim, which was partly upheld by the Aboriginal land commissioner, John Toohey, who awarded the claim for the country north and east of Uluru but concluded that because "Ayers Rock and the Olgas" were within the national park, they were not unalienated Crown land and were therefore excluded from the claim. Nonetheless, Toohey argued, both sites were clearly of "enormous significance for Aboriginal people." The decision only intensified the Anangu's determination to lodge a successful claim for Uluru and Kata Tjuta.

In 1983, the newly elected Hawke Labor government was keen to avoid placing responsibility for the management of Uluru in the hands of the Northern Territory government, which remained hostile to Aboriginal land rights. Hawke decided to intervene and return the Ayers Rock–Mount Olga National Park to Aboriginal ownership and management. The question of why the government wanted to grant the Anangu freehold title of the park was clearly answered in the cabinet submission by Barry Cohen, minister for Aboriginal affairs: to "provide an alternative source [of revenue and employment] for Aboriginal people . . . [and] continued management of the area as a national park . . . [including] protection of sites of particular significance to Aboriginal women." The rapid development of tourism infrastructure—the Yulara tourist village opened in 1984, and bus and camping tours gave way to jet airlines as domestic and international tourists arrived in ever larger numbers—now walked hand in hand with the Anangu's struggle for justice.

One of those sites of significance was the cave near Mutitjulu Waterhole, where the drawings on the walls had first transfixed Charles Mountford in 1935. And in several of the submissions made to the government, McKinnon's shooting of Yokununna and Paddy's subsequent flight and exile from his homeland formed a crucial component of the Anangu's case for the handback of their land. This much was acknowledged by Justice Toohey himself:

> In 1934, while investigating the death of a young Aboriginal man near Attila (Mt Conner), the police arrested several men who later escaped and made their way to Uluru.

There they hid at Mutitjulu but were found. One, a brother of Paddy Uluru, tried to escape and was shot. The death is still in people's minds. I have no doubt that the conflict (between black and white) that did exist, in particular the punitive expeditions, caused people to move away from actual or potential trouble.

Innocent people fled the threat of violence. McKinnon's callous act was *the* foundational moment in a long history of injustice, as campfire stories were recorded of how the rock's "number one" custodian, Paddy Uluru, had been driven from his Country. After five decades, the true impact of the shooting on the Anangu had finally been conveyed to the seat of power in Canberra, underwriting the case for the return of Uluru to its traditional owners.

Paddy Uluru's sons, Reggie and Cassidy, who were both heavily involved in the campaign leading up to the handback, were present at Uluru on October 26, 1985, when Governor-General Sir Ninian Stephen presented the Anangu with the title deeds to the Ayers Rock–Mount Olga National Park. Reggie stood next to elder Nipper Winmati when he received the framed document from the governor-general to the delight of the crowd. Much later, Rene Kulitja, artist and elder of the Mutitjulu community, recalled the occasion: "Everyone was dancing and singing. We were so happy that we got our land back."

David Roberts's 1986 film, *Uluru: An Anangu Story*, captured the exhilaration and extraordinary rush of optimism that accompanied the event. The Anangu had always returned to Uluru for their ceremonies, and now they had legal confirmation that their connection to their land had never been lost. A succession of elders spoke on camera, demanding that white Australians respect Anangu law and culture: "We think that we should be listened to more. . . . We are the only ones who really understand this place"; "It is the spirit of the

Anangu that is in that rock, not the white man"; "We've been given our Aboriginal spirit. . . . Uluru and Kata Tjuta are safe at last."

Like most of white Australia, Sir Ninian Stephen could only glimpse the significance of this moment for the Anangu. Joseph Donald, the last Aboriginal survivor of the terrible events in 1934 and the senior custodian of Bloods Range near Docker River, traveled from his home to be present for the ceremony. It was remarkable that not far from the spot where McKinnon had shot Yokununna fifty years earlier, Paddy Uluru's two sons stood as esteemed leaders while one of the other men McKinnon had hunted, Donald, watched on, all of them witness to the handback of land the whites had so long assumed was theirs for the taking.

As Sir Ninian approached the microphone to speak, surrounded by Aboriginal flags and WELCOME TO ABORIGINAL LAND posters, a light plane flew overhead, trailing the banner AYERS ROCK FOR ALL AUSTRALIANS. Resistance to the handback in the Territory was strong, with both the government and opposition resenting the idea that "one single group" be given exclusive ownership of Uluru, although the agreement ensured that the national park would be leased back to the Commonwealth for ninety-nine years and jointly managed by the Anangu and the national parks service. The aerial protest was the brainchild of Peter Severin, the owner of Curtin Springs Station, who had built many of the early structures at Uluru, including, in 1963, the chain that thousands of tourists would use to scale the rock until the climb was closed in October 2019. Severin was also an old friend of Bill McKinnon's.

Neither the protest in the sky nor the thinly disguised contempt of Territory politicians, who argued that the Anangu were a "false tribe" who had no right to own Uluru, could dampen the euphoria of the handback. "Today," Sir Ninian Stephen told the crowd, "we stand not merely in the center of our continent but at its very heart. We stand beside what has become one of our national symbols, to

Aboriginal people—Uluru—to others, Ayers Rock." He reflected on the rock's "deep spiritual significance," its roots, he said, going back to "time immemorial."

As recently as the 1940s, few non-Aboriginal people had set foot anywhere in central Australia, let alone visited Uluru. In less than fifty years, the rock had gone from a lonely monolith that barely registered in the national imagination to the most recognizable symbol of Australia next to the Sydney Opera House and the kangaroo. What had long been the Anangu's "holy place" and "most sacred spot" had gradually become the entire nation's center, at once geographical and spiritual.

During the last decades of the twentieth century, Uluru was branded one of Australia's major tourist destinations, a place in the Western Desert to which thousands of visitors from around the world flew or drove, for a few hours or days to "listen and learn" about Anangu culture and, often, to climb the rock. One of those climbers was Bill McKinnon.

In 1984, a "Back to Ayers Rock" "get together" was planned as a last hurrah for the "old-timers" before the handback occurred. Never one to miss a reunion, McKinnon returned to the Territory in March that year, logging his daily activities in minute detail, as if he were still out on patrol, although this time with considerably more creature comforts. "Left home . . . for Brisbane airport at 4:45 am. . . . Boarded flight 250 (Ansett) at 8:30 am. Breakfast after leaving Brisbane consisted of bacon, omelet, mushrooms, rolls, butter and jam, tea, orange juice." Picked up at Alice Springs by his old friend Peter Severin, and greeted by many people who remembered him, he soon found himself standing at the Roadhouse bar at Curtin Springs, where he "started to move into old [Territory] habits."

Mark McAdie, former police assistant commissioner in the Northern Territory, was stationed at Mutitjulu. When he heard that Bill McKinnon was making a trip out to the rock, he thought he'd mention it to some of the older Aboriginal men who might remember him. But when he relayed the news to Yankunytjatjara elder Toby Naninga, the man blanched. Soon afterward, Naninga disappeared. He stayed away from Uluru for three months, returning long after McKinnon had come and gone. "Why did you leave?" McAdie asked him when he finally came back. "It was no accident," Naninga replied, without revealing that he was one of the men McKinnon had chased to the rock in 1934. Toby Naninga was also Paddy Uluru's brother. The mere mention of McKinnon's name had caused him to flee.

The morning after he arrived, McKinnon took the opportunity to fly with Severin in a Cessna "210 single engine" to deliver supplies of "frozen beef and rabbits" to Docker River. He was there for all of fifteen minutes, just enough time to offload the meat. Docker River, of course, was the home of Joseph Donald, the youngest of the four escaped prisoners he'd chased to the rock fifty years earlier. Little did McKinnon realize that he would have had to walk only a few hundred yards to find him. It was the closest they had come to being in each other's presence since 1934. On the return leg of the flight, he looked down on the red sandhills and remembered the "epic manhunt." "[We] changed course to fly over the new 'Yulara' township and low over Ayers Rock; arrived back at station at 3:30 pm, after one of the most interesting, satisfying and pleasing trips that I have ever had. I took two snaps of Lake Amadeus, about 40 miles north from Ayers Rock, and along which I traveled with camels while looking for escaped murderers in October 1934."

The next morning, marveling at the "many buses, cars and trucks" that were refueling at Curtin Springs "enroute to Ayers Rock," he "had a good walk in the sandhills for exercise" and drove out to visit the grave of Ellis M. Bankin, the motorcyclist "who perished . . . about 15 miles east from Mount Conner in January 1936." Bankin had intended to travel via Ayers Rock and the Petermann and

Rawlinson Ranges to Western Australia. McKinnon's was the last home at which he called before leaving Alice Springs. "We tried . . . to stop him," he lamented, "but without success. I have always remembered Doreen giving him some apple cucumbers from our garden to take with him. He was later tracked and found dead, with petrol in his petrol tank, and also water in a container." The lonely death of this young white schoolteacher moved McKinnon deeply.

That evening, he attended "an official dinner for 'pioneers,'" with a special guest, Paul Everingham, chief minister of the Northern Territory. McKinnon proudly noted his own preeminence: "Bill McKinnon was one of only two names mentioned—credited with being the first white man to climb Mount Olga. A dance followed the dinner, it was the funniest and wildest dance I have ever seen. It lasted till 4 am but I retired at 1:30 am." He listened as speeches of "sorrow" were delivered, bemoaning the handback of Uluru. As he wrote defiantly in his journal, "By government decision, the whole block of buildings near the Rock is to be handed over to the blacks—and the town of Yulara, several miles north from Mt. Olga, will be the European center. It may reasonably be anticipated that there will be a series of mysterious fires, as the residents are unanimous that the blacks will never get these buildings. Asked for comment, I gave my whole hearted approval to such accidents."

The following morning, March 11, at the age of eighty-one, fifty-two years after he bathed in the rockpool on the summit, he climbed the rock with Peter Severin. What had taken him forty minutes up and back as a young man was now an ordeal: "This time it took 2 and a half hours up and 1 and a half down again. It was a hot day, I had no hat and was well cooked in the process. I do not intend to climb it anymore." Severin took a photograph of McKinnon at the summit, capturing a man who posed as master of all he surveyed, his hands on the bronze plaque with its directional compass, like a captain at the wheel of his ship.

Bill McKinnon on top of Uluru, 1984

Whether or not McKinnon visited Mutitjulu Waterhole, or "Maggie Springs" as he remembered it, on that day, he failed to say. In any case, he had no regrets. When he was asked by a Darwin journalist three years earlier to reflect on the "case that almost cost him his life and his career," he replied that he "felt exonerated" and "wouldn't have done anything differently." "I believed in the law," he said emphatically, "and I still do." For McKinnon, the Aboriginal men he'd hunted mercilessly across the sandhills would always be "prisoners" and "murderers."

The climb up the rock had exhausted him and he needed a "quiet day" to recover. "Wrote ten 'I've climbed Ayers Rock' postcards . . . strolling in sandhills, stubbying, reminiscing with old hands." A few days later, he drove back to Alice Springs with Severin, picking up a Japanese cyclist whose bike had broken down along the way. On arrival, he was taken straight to the Police Club, where twenty men awaited him for a surprise reception. They shared XXXX-brand beers in "stubbies"—375-milliliter bottles, a long-standing popular choice among his peers. It would be the first of several events to celebrate his return to the Territory, including a visit to the Rifle Club he had founded in 1933, where members now competed annually for the "W. McKinnon Championship," and a barbecue at the Police Club, where more than one hundred people were gathered in his honor.

Wandering around town for the first time in twenty years, he was "very disappointed." "The friendly atmosphere seems to be gone," he thought, "and I could find no place to get a malted milk. Even the John Flynn church had dirty looking blacks loafing around on the lawns, and no sign of any service." Shortly afterward, he flew home to Queensland, after "one long whale of a time," pleased to be back on his "own dunghill," but already certain he would return for the centenary of policing in central Australia in 1986. When a local newspaper ran a story on his climb up the rock, he clipped the page and sent it to his daughter, Susan: "Next week I hope to get prints from some of my recent color slides . . . hope to send or give you one of me—standing at the cairn on top of Ayers Rock. . . . Love and best wishes to all, Dad."

In May that year, McKinnon met his second love, Olga Brown, a former secretary at Queensland Newspapers, and by December they were married. It was nine years after Doreen's death, and Brisbane's *Sunday Mail* considered the marriage a newsworthy event. The *Mail*'s story, replete with remarks about a "sprightly Bill McKinnon" marrying a woman twelve years his junior, managed to reduce the wedding to a mere sideshow compared to his former policing exploits in central Australia—MATRIMONIAL KNOT IS ANOTHER ADVENTURE FOR "HANGING BILL." McKinnon explained how he was given the sobriquet: "Someone played a joke on me by leaving a noose in my office one day, but I never used it."

When he returned in April 1986 for what would be his final visit to the Territory, he was one of many former policemen who had traveled from around Australia for the occasion. A trip out to the country where he began his first camel patrols proved irresistible, especially when the journey from Alice Springs to Ayers Rock, which took him three trying weeks in the 1930s, could now be experienced in air-conditioned comfort in little more than five hours. When the police centenary celebrations were done, he headed out to Uluru.

"In 1986 [Olga] and I went to the Alice for a celebration of a police presence of one hundred years in the center, and we got on a bus in the Alice in the morning; we went to Ayers Rock; had a look at the rock; my wife climbed about twenty feet up it just so she could say she was on Ayers Rock; and we had lunch at the Yulara Hotel, which didn't exist in my camel days, and got back to Alice Springs the same night." At the age of eighty-four, McKinnon's life had borne witness to the remarkable transformation of Uluru in the Australian imagination. The man who shot the brother of Uluru's "number one" custodian in one of the defining moments of central Australia's frontier had returned to the same site five decades later as yet another tourist.

As he sat lunching with his wife at the Yulara Hotel, McKinnon had no idea that weeks earlier, only a few hours' drive away, at Docker River, Joseph Donald had told his version of the events at Uluru in 1934 to documentary filmmaker David Batty, who was then living in Alice Springs and beginning what would turn out to be a long and distinguished career making films with and for Aboriginal people.

Donald had witnessed every moment of what took place near Mutitjulu Waterhole. Like Paddy Uluru, he stayed away from Uluru for two decades, living most of his life at the settlement at Docker River, where he was one of the senior elders. In 1978, he officially welcomed Governor-General Zelman Cowen to his Country. In 1986, David Batty was at Docker River when Joseph Donald unexpectedly took him aside.

> I was at Docker River filming something quite unrelated. [Joseph] walked me to a spot on the edge of the community and we sat down and he told me that story. My

Pitjantjatjara was pretty thin at that time and I really didn't know what he was talking about, but it seemed important to him that he told me and that I filmed it. I was blown away when we had it translated.

Batty didn't broadcast the film of Donald telling his story until 2016, when a chance encounter led him to ask Donald's family if they would grant permission for him to upload it online. "I was working in Alice and got a young bloke from the rock to do some voice work and Joseph's story came up [in conversation]. I told him I had a film with him recounting that story. He was so excited as his good mate is Joseph's grandson. So I asked the family if I could put it up on YouTube and they were only too happy for that." The story that Donald had told countless times to the "Uluru and Docker River mobs" could now be seen by every Australian. In January 2022, little more than five thousand people had viewed the video.

It is a bracing eyewitness account of the "killing times," told with drama and humor. Sitting on the ground in shorts and a T-shirt, his mop of gray hair set off by the bright red band of initiated men, Donald both speaks and choreographs the story, drawing circles and lines in the sand to pinpoint this place or that, raising his index finger to emphasize a point, alternately conducting, humming, laughing, and holding his head in his hands as he moves from one tortured memory to the next (www.youtube.com/watch?v=1TN2IFgIcEI).

> *At Wallara Ranch [145 miles northeast of Uluru] a policeman chased me and got me. He put handcuffs on me and took me from Wallara Ranch, that way [pointing] still with handcuffs on. I was a prisoner in the old days. We had no idea. Just bush people. Poor buggers [laughs].*
>
> *We kept on walking, walking, walking. I was thinking to myself, "What's going on?" There were four of us. I'm the only*

one still alive. We were chained up at night. The policeman's name was McKinnon. There was another policeman and Carbine [police tracker]. Those three were taking us around handcuffed. We kept on going. It was really hot. We got burned. They let us rest in the shade and they made us a cup of tea. It was really hot in the sun. We sweated a lot, us poor buggers. They gave us tea, we drank the tea and felt better.

We left there and went to Bob Buck's station [Middleton Ponds]. That old man used to live there. We turned up there and he took us to his place. We were still handcuffed. We sat down and talked and talked. McKinnon asked me questions but I didn't know because I was innocent. I didn't understand English. Then he took my handcuffs off and tied the others up to a tree. I was lying down. I was a young fella then.

That night I was lying there thinking. Then somebody threw sand at me and said, "Hey." When I opened my eyes, the others had run away. I didn't know what was going on so I got up and ran away too [laughs]. . . . We jumped over a cliff and landed on top of each other [laughs again]. We laid there for a while, it was a dark night with no moon. We kept going then we slowed down and made camp.

We woke up really early before dawn. . . . We were really frightened and didn't know what was going on. We forgot about the policemen and just kept running, running. We made another camp and drank at Ulanga soakage. We had to dig it out. In the morning we had a big drink at the soakage. . . . I wanted us to go up to Wallara Ranch but we kept on going west, going, going, going. It rained so we made a fire and sat in a windbreak. We made little hunting sticks so we could dig up perenti [goannas]. We killed lots of perenti. There were puddles of water. We cooked the perenti and moved on. . . . We were at that old place near Uluru. We stayed there for a few days eating perenti.

The police . . . came to Wallara Ranch on camels looking for us. There they got horses and started following our tracks. That old man Carbine was with them. They were following our tracks. . . . After walking all day I was just about to make a campfire. Not with matches but with a firestick. Then I heard [imitates the sound of neighing horses]. It was a horse with that old man [Carbine] on it. I stopped and listened, then I saw the horse coming. I ripped off my clothes and threw them away. Then put out the fire and [raising his arm] took off.

The horses were galloping along toward us. I ran over a sandhill and hid. The horses got to the sandhill, split up and went along the base of the sandhill in both directions. I ran back the same way the horses had just come. Then I heard a rifle shot. A policeman [Police Paddy] and Carbine. Those two, they found my tracks and started chasing me. I stopped and thought, "There's a lot of spinifex here." I pulled the spinifex out, sat down and covered myself with it [raises his arm]. The horses went right over me and kept going. They didn't see me. The horse jumped over me. I stayed there till the afternoon. The police were still looking around for me but I was in the spinifex. Then they took off looking for the others. So I took off all the spinifex and got up. I went off into the night and saw the police horses in front of me. I kept on going. I picked up a stick to hit Carbine and the policemen [chuckles]. I made a noise so I ran off. I ran toward that airstrip at Ayers Rock and went into the scrub. I couldn't have a fire so I dug a hole to sleep in. . . .

In the morning I was up before daybreak. I went toward Inintitjara and had a drink of water there. I sat down and had a think for a while and looked around me. One of the others turned up to drink at the waterhole. I waited till he had a drink before I spoke to him. Then I joined him. Those others have passed away now. I'm the only one still alive. The three of us got together and went around the rock. We kept on going.

We came over a rock and saw our friend who had been shot by those bad men. A .44 bullet went through his chest and tore out his side. He walked toward us. We got him by the arm, poor bugger. We put him in a cave to look after him. He was my brother-in-law. We have the same grandfather.

While I was looking after him, my grandfather said, "Climb up that slippery part of the rock." I climbed up there so I could see the policeman—McKinnon. I sat down watching, watching. I got shivers up the back and felt something funny. I thought my nephew [Carbine] must have been thinking about me. But then I heard the camel walking. Then I saw it. A man on it said, "Come down from there. I've seen you." He spoke Yankunytjatjara because he was a Yankunytjatjara man. He called me but I didn't come down. He got out his rifle (imitates rifle sound) and loaded it. Then he fired it at me. He missed me. Then he fired again. I looked up and saw all the rocks rolling down toward me. Then McKinnon started running toward me with two rifles. I was sitting there wondering what to do— shall I go down? So I jumped down and landed on the sand. I stood up and I saw the police running toward me. So I laid down. The police came and looked around. . . . I was really lucky laying down without being seen. I held my breath.

The policemen went into the cave. They found the one who had been shot. They grabbed him by the arm and brought him outside. They asked my brother-in-law, "Where are the other three?" [He] didn't tell the police where the others were. So they shot him. The police shot him in front of me. There was no Native Affairs or Welfare or government there. In my presence they shot him [pointing to his forehead]. I started crying but only tears. After crying I went into the cave and was feeling around. I felt the other two and really started crying. I cried myself to sleep. I woke up and started talking to them. They told me to get out and go because it was getting dark and the crickets had started talking. We came out of the cave and saw water running down the rock. I looked up to see if there were any clouds but there was only one little one. So it was like a miracle just for me. I laid down for a while and thought this is day-time.

I fell asleep and when I woke up it was nighttime again. The moon had just come up. I looked around and saw the police-man looking up the rock. It was as though he was looking at me. So I came round the side of the rock behind him. He was still looking up for me so he could shoot me. I came out where that water and bush tucker fig is. I came out that way and ran. The other two came out and ran away as well [draws in the sand] where that one rock is. We met there and ran toward Kata Tjuta.

We kept running fast till we got to Mount Olga. We sat down watching, watching, still couldn't see the policemen. They must have found our tracks again. "Here's their tracks. This is where they must have got away." We weren't watching for a while. Then when we looked we saw them coming. It was in the afternoon. We got up and ran. . . . They were still looking for us on horses. . . . We were stepping on spinifex clumps. No tracks. We kept on going. They must have been looking for us back there. We climbed to the top of a hill and sat down, watch-ing, watching. We were looking back but couldn't see the police-men. It got late while we were watching, so we camped there.

In the morning we were still sitting there. No womera. No spears. No hunting stick. We were sitting down really hungry, watching, watching. We got down, had a drink of water and took off. We saw a big [echidna]. A really big one. It had its back toward us. We killed it, cleaned it, cooked it and ate it. We were happy then because we had something to eat. . . . We went on to Waltanta and camped there.

I said to my grandfather, "Let me go from here on my own now, I'll go straight to that place." He told me not to go and started crying, but I grabbed a fire stick and ran away. I ran away by myself. As I was running I was crying for the other two. My grandfather was asking me to go to Aparatjara [laughs].

I was running along by myself. I saw some water in a rock hole and drank it. . . . I kept on running, I was a young fella then, so I could run fast. It got dark there so I made camp. That night I heard little dingo pups so I threw rocks at them. I thought the dingoes might bite me. They might be cheeky.

The birds woke me up in the morning. I took off again and when I arrived at Utjutja I saw a person in the distance looking up a gum tree for maku [witchetty grubs]. Then I saw another man up in the tree. I walked toward them but they didn't see me. Then I sat down and said to them, "Excuse me." They looked at me and started crying for me. I was naked, no trousers. Nothing. Naked. We walked back to their camp and everyone started crying for me. Women were falling to the ground everywhere. All my mothers. I stayed there for a while. They cooked me a feed of damper and tea. I sneaked away again on my own. . . . I had a drink of water and a swim. Then I came . . . past here [turns his head]—Docker River. And kept going that way. West [draws in the sand]. I arrived at a place with a lot of whitefellas [Giles, eastern Western Australia], that whitefella mob who came in with the army. They [family] saw me as I turned up. . . . My aunty was there. She asked me to go over to her and she started crying. She took me and put me

*in the shade, cooked me stew. I was really skinny [laughs],
didn't look like a strong healthy man. I was skinny and weak
because I hadn't eaten any meat. I was thinking to myself, "I've
had a really hard time." They gave me some soup and I was
eating it with a spoon. Young girls gave me damper and they
were crying too. I didn't look like a really strong man. I got really skinny, poor bugger.*

*I sat there till the afternoon. I thought, "I'm going to get
that Carbine and [Paddy]." He's a Ngaatjatjara bloke. Pintupi. Ngaatjatjara. The others said they were going to
shoot him.*

*After I had eaten, they gave me a new blanket they bought
in the big town. They told me to camp in the middle of them. I
slept in the middle [laughs]. They gave me 50/50 flour, matches
and sugar. Then they started on their way. They said, "That's
your blanket now." They told me to stay in the hills, not to come
out of the hills [points]. Then they went on to Warakurna with
those whitefellas.*

*I went and stayed at Wallara. I never saw the police again.
I was the winner.*

Told more than fifty years after the shooting, Donald's account is
astonishingly vivid. Despite the harrowing nature of this experience,
he manages to emerge victorious in the end—"I was the winner"—
evading and outsmarting his pursuers at every turn. Not only did he
have to dodge McKinnon's and Carbine's bullets; he also had to out-
run armed men riding horses and camels. We can almost feel his
elation. He continued to look for the possibility of revenge, both at
the time and long afterward. He reveals that one of his pursuers,
Carbine, was also related to him. And it powerfully contradicts
McKinnon's account, which makes no mention of the final shot

outside the cave. Donald, the last surviving Aboriginal witness, is the voice that was never heard in the board of inquiry's report.

The sequence of events is clear. Two of the escapees were in the cave near Mutitjulu Waterhole with Yokununna. They had placed him there not only to hide but because he was already badly wounded and exhausted. Donald, who was outside, did not see McKinnon fire into the cave, but he saw what happened after McKinnon and Carbine dragged Yokununna out. McKinnon, he claimed, shot Yokununna (again) when he refused to reveal the whereabouts of the others. It was not self-defense. He shot him at point-blank range, enraged because he could not force Yokununna to betray his friends. Together with his trackers, Paddy and Carbine, he then proceeded to hunt for the others without success.

Donald's telling, which echoes the "clever man" narrative common in Anangu oral history, is by far the most detailed account recorded. It's also one of many renditions that have been told by Anangu since the 1950s. Sometimes McKinnon's name is not even mentioned. Sometimes the reasons for him arresting the men are veiled or ignored entirely. Names and details vary in every account. Some claim that on the night of the shooting, McKinnon and Carbine were almost killed as they slept, the opportunity for payback thwarted at the last minute when a horse stirred. Others talk of McKinnon and his trackers trying to smoke the men out of the cave, or of sacred objects that were in the men's possession being hidden there before they fled. Some fail to mention the trial and conviction of Numberlin and Nangee. As Jen Cowley writes in *I Am Uluru*, although the shooting of Yokununna is undoubtedly a "seminal moment" in Uluru's history, "the story has shifted shape, not so as to rewrite history but to protect it." Nor does the story feature in any of the interpretative panels that stand near Mutitjulu Waterhole today, which focus on the larger cultural significance of the site for Anangu.

The law that has bound Uluru's custodians for thousands of years still applies. As ever, more is withheld from whitefellas than is revealed to them.

Joseph Donald died several years after telling David Batty his story. Paddy Uluru, who met Donald in a tearful reunion at Uluru in the 1950s, died before him, in 1979.

PART THREE

SONGS OF THE CENTER

Albert Namatjira, *Greetings from South West Patrol*, 1932

8

SHOT TO HIT

McKinnon returned to Buderim in Queensland and lived out the last years of his retirement, "looked up to," along with other policemen from the Territory's early days, as a member of an elite group: "men among men." Convinced that he'd had "a more varied series of adventures than that experienced by the average man," he continued to tell stories of his first camel patrols well into his early nineties. He died in Buderim in 1997, four weeks short of his ninety-fifth birthday. His contribution to the history of central Australia was acknowledged by the Northern Territory Police Force in a special tribute edition of its historical journal, *Citation*. Obituaries in *The Australian* and local newspapers lauded him as a man who "exemplified the tact, resourcefulness, courage and compassion that police work required." He was "one of the Territory's historical treasures."

Dedicated to McKinnon's memory, his daughter, Susan, joined the Retired Police Association of the Northern Territory in 1999 and received a Police Service Medal for McKinnon's thirty years of service on his behalf. In July 2019, searching for her name online, I came across an image of a piece she'd donated to the Queensland Art

Gallery in 2004. The artwork opened a door in my investigation of Yokununna's killing.

In 1932, when McKinnon visited Hermannsburg Mission on his first camel patrol, he met Arrernte artist Albert Namatjira, who would become one of the most famous Aboriginal artists in Australia. McKinnon commissioned Namatjira to make one dozen oval mulga wood plaques—GREETINGS FROM SOUTH WEST PATROL—showing his camel train marching through the spinifex and sand, for which he paid Namatjira five shillings each. These disarmingly simple pokerwork engravings, aglow in the colors of the country, were some of Namatjira's first commissioned artworks, made with the encouragement of the Lutheran missionary Pastor Friedrich Albrecht. McKinnon leads the camel train, his tracker at the rear. Seen today, with the knowledge of subsequent events, the seemingly innocuous image on the plaques bristles with darker implications.

Born in the same year (1902), the two men were introduced to each other by Albrecht, who had already noticed the young Namatjira's "artistic inclinations," encouraged as they were by the artist Rex Battarbee, who mounted an exhibition of his own landscapes at Hermannsburg in the same year and would return several times in the 1930s before moving to central Australia permanently in 1940. Albrecht was intent on "commercializing" Aboriginal art produced on the mission, and McKinnon was probably encouraged to invest. But his decision to commission Namatjira showed again that he was acutely aware of the historical significance of his first patrols. He was both eager to memorialize his presence and willing to pay Namatjira handsomely for his artistic skill. Years later, when he claimed that he was a "friend of the natives," he might well have regarded his commissioning of Namatjira as one example.

The plaque was interesting in itself, but it also opened another door: the gallery listed the donor's name as Susan Golledge—McKinnon's daughter's married name, which I'd not known before.

Aware that she was born in 1939, I couldn't be sure that she was still alive. But at least her surname was uncommon. I searched the white pages directory. Fortunately, there were only four entries for an "S. Golledge." On the fourth and final call I found her living in a suburb of Brisbane, aged eighty and recently diagnosed with dementia. Susan was warm and helpful on the phone. Understandably cursing the "cruel disease" that had suddenly announced its arrival, she was pleased to have the opportunity to talk about "Dad" before her health declined. She told me how, as a teenager, she'd been introduced to Police Paddy and had served Albert Namatjira in the Commonwealth Bank at Alice Springs, where she worked for a while as a teller—"He'd come in and place his mark on the piece of paper." As for Dad, "he was lucid to the end," she said proudly. She was his only child and she thought the world of her father. "If you're interested," she offered, "I've got boxes of his things in the garage, and you're welcome to go through them if you want."

Within a week I was on a plane to Brisbane. Merely to hear her utter the word "Dad" was enough to unsettle me. I was uncertain how much she knew or wanted to know, and I was doubtful about how much I should tell her. Her recollection of Police Paddy appeared entirely unencumbered by his reputation for unbridled cruelty and violence. Like the image of McKinnon on the mulga plaque, the anecdote made him appear as yet another benign connection to the "pioneer days" of central Australia.

Susan lived around twelve miles from Brisbane's central business district, but the drive there along the freeway seemed longer. The house stood on a corner in a relatively new suburb, probably built in the 1970s. Nearby was an all-too-familiar landscape—KFC, Woolworths, Caltex, and McDonald's—it could easily have been anywhere in Australia. When I walked up the drive and knocked on the door, Susan was waiting for me. We sat down in the living room for a few minutes before she walked me out to the garage. One of

Bill McKinnon's Brisbane garage archive

Albert Namatjira's SOUTH WEST PATROL plaques hung proudly in the hallway; an inscription on the back of the plaque left no doubt as to its provenance: "1. Made by Albert: Hermannsburg"; photos of "Doreen and Bill" stood on the mantelpiece, and at the foot of the dining table, three suitcases waited, full of McKinnon's photographs and slides that Susan and Ian, her son, had kindly left out for me to go through. Close by, framed landscapes painted by Oscar Namatjira (Albert's second son) and Henoch Raberaba—more works from the Hermannsburg school collected by McKinnon—leaned against the wall. Susan seemed surprised to learn how much I already knew about her father's life. "He was very good at documenting things," she said, smiling.

As soon as we entered the garage, this became abundantly clear. There, in the corner, under plastic pots, empty food coolers (or eskies as Australians call them), and assorted clutter, were metal trunks and wooden boxes full of documents and memorabilia of every description: McKinnon's entire library of books on central Australia, many of them personally inscribed by the authors, his schoolbooks, his will, his legal and financial records, Masonic Lodge paraphernalia, his family history and memoirs, a lifetime's correspondence, boxes of slides taken on family holidays, and nearly every Marilyn Monroe film on reel-to-reel. It was an unexpectedly rich find. The bottom trunk—difficult to prize open because it had been shut for so long—contained the gold: his press cuttings and every original logbook from the early 1930s until he died in 1997.

McKinnon had continued to log every day of his life. After thirty years' policing in central and northern Australia, the habit of recording proved difficult to break. No matter how mundane, he logged the day's activities with a detailed realism reminiscent of James Joyce's novel *Ulysses*: "7.12.72, Changed all wheels around. (Tire no. 'WPOM2772' was staked at Nambour Showground on 6.7.72) have now put it with a tube on off-side back wheel"; "10/12/85, Digging in S.W. part of garden, after clearing all cultivated parts of weeds;" "4/1/89, Usual shopping trip in A.M. Mowed in p.m." When he left Alice Springs, "having ceased active Police Service in the Northern Territory Police Force on 21st December 1961 and commenced accumulated recreation leave prior to retirement on 16th June 1962," he drove a station wagon full of his belongings about one and a half thousand miles to his father's house in Nambour, moving through everything from grasshopper plagues to dust storms and impassable wet roads. The journal he kept along the way again showed his obsessive attention to detail with a Queensland twist: "16.3.62, Bought three pineapples and a bunch of bananas near Beerwah" . . . "18.3.62, threw one pineapple away."

On patrol during his years in the Territory, he'd always been careful to log the details of his assistance to stranded travelers. In retirement, he monitored his neighbors in Buderim, ferrying his carless neighbor's visiting relatives on sightseeing and shopping trips and to numerous "counter lunches": "15.9.78, took M.&W. Ivers & J. Hargreaves—two on crutches & one with stiff knees—to the Chelsea flower show at Nambour." The ministering policeman whose razor-like attention to detail and knowledge of the country saved several European lives in central Australia never retired.

As I searched through every box and trunk in the garage, Susan stood and watched, occasionally asking questions or making comments. "I'm very proud of my dad. He was such a wonderful father and a good man. . . . If he was looking down on us now, he'd be so pleased that you're here." A neighbor dropped in to make sure Susan was "okay with this strange man." Her youngest son, Matt, called by to meet me. Everyone in the family couldn't have been more helpful. I asked Susan a few questions and she recounted finer details with photographic recall—American soldiers driving through Tennant Creek during the war in their jeeps, throwing oranges to children on the roadside—but the larger shape of her memories, understandably, seemed to be fading. When I asked her about the board of inquiry's 1935 report, she looked bewildered.

"I don't know anything about that."

By the time I'd worked my way through the material, including the suitcases of photographs (several albums of McKinnon's original photographs from Rabaul in the 1920s and his camel patrols in the early 1930s), I knew that I would have to return. In the rush of opening and closing so many boxes, I was fearful I'd missed something. That night, flying back to Sydney, I marveled at how McKinnon had kept everything, archiving every mention of his name in books, police journals, and the press—"see p. 26"—much of it meticulously filed and dated, sometimes with explicit instructions or interpolations: "save," "keep," "incorrect," "what rot!" His desire to be present in history was insatiable. Yet in all his attention to record keeping, silences abounded. The 1935 board of inquiry's report was nowhere to be found in his mass of papers, nor one press clipping related to it. There were a few examples of summaries by others who glossed over the report's findings, but nothing of substance. After his death, most of his local obituarists continued in the same vein, averting their eyes

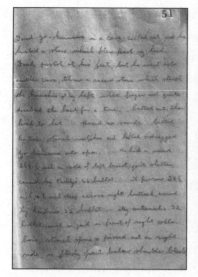

Bill McKinnon's patrol journal

from the events of 1934. But that afternoon in the garage, in the bottom of the trunk that held his logbooks, I found one piece of evidence that I had never expected to find.

It was one of his original logbooks from the early 1930s, except that this particular book, its cover crinkled and worn with age, its back pages crammed with lists of books to be read ("sometime!"), was *the* one he'd used at Uluru in 1934, only hours after he shot Yokununna.

In the 1930s, police patrol records in the Northern Territory were kept "for a short time and then destroyed," unless the silverfish had already done the job, yet another reason this find was remarkable. I realized then that McKinnon had used this journal as the basis of a second, handwritten account in another logbook, before typing up a third and final version for his superiors and the board of inquiry. Compared with the last two accounts, McKinnon's record of the shooting in his first log differed in one crucial respect. In his evidence to the 1935 inquiry he maintained that he had fired at Yokununna "without taking aim": "Taking a quick glimpse I saw him facing me and picking up another stone. Keeping my head clear, I pointed the pistol in his direction [*without taking any aim*] whatever, and fired a second shot." Yet only hours after the event, he recorded the following entry in the first log: "Fired pistol at his feet, but he went into another cave, threw a second stone which struck the knuckle of my left index finger and quite disabled the hand for a time. Called out, then [*fired to hit*]. Heard no sound." McKinnon then proceeded to meticulously document what happened after he fired his pistol.

> Called Carbine, struck matches, and lifted & dragged Yokununna into open. He had a wound 2 and a half × one and a half inch on side of left breast, quite shallow, caused by Paddy's .44 bullet. A furrow 2 × half inch & half inch deep across right buttock, caused by Carbine's .22 bullet. My automatic .22 bullet went in just in front of right collar bone, struck spine & passed out on right side, in fleshy part below shoulder blade. This paralyzed him. With great difficulty we carried and lowered him 40 feet down to level ground, where he died three hours later. Paddy & party arrived. Numberlin & Wong-We dug grave & buried their mate.

McKinnon's account differed significantly from the testimony of Joseph Donald, who claimed that he saw McKinnon drag Yokununna out of the cave and shoot him at point-blank range when he failed to reveal the whereabouts of the other escapees. Yet even by his own account at the time of the shooting, let alone Donald's testimony, McKinnon had lied to the inquiry. He aimed and fired at Yokununna.

Although he donated some of his photographs and recollections to the Northern Territory Archives in 1991, he left his original police logbooks stored in his Buderim garage. He could easily have discarded the original 1934 journal that proved he was lying to the board of inquiry, but he chose not to do so. Perhaps his irrepressible instinct for documentary preservation—he had also started researching a history of policing in the Northern Territory—overrode his desire to protect his posthumous reputation. Either that or he had forgotten the words "I fired to hit" existed and had come to believe his own fictions. For the moment, I said nothing about this to Susan or any member of her family.

On August 15, 2019, I flew to Brisbane for the second time to slowly comb through McKinnon's correspondence and photographs. I was sitting in the dining room of Susan's home after I'd finished working my way through his papers when I noticed a missed call on my phone. It was an Adelaide number. Within minutes I was speaking with Anna Russo, Aboriginal heritage and repatriation manager at the South Australian Museum. Yokununna's remains were there. His name was "inked" on his skull: YOCKANUNNA [sic] COMPLETE SKELETON. Cleland had taken the remains back with him on the train to Adelaide, where he deposited them with the university in a collection of human skeletal remains until this collection was transferred to the South Australian Museum in 2017. Over the years, Yokununna's skull had been separated from his postcranial remains, which may reside today with other unprovenanced remains in the museum's Keeping Place or else were lost or discarded. On the table next to me as I spoke to the museum were McKinnon's photographs of his patrols and the logbook he'd kept at Uluru in 1934.

By the end of 2019 tourists were no longer allowed to climb Uluru. The impending closure of the climb at Uluru was making international news, and the Commonwealth government's slow response to Indigenous leaders' demands for justice and truth-telling was coming under increasing criticism.

The story I'd been tracking for two years seemed to have its own internal teleology.

McKinnon was part of two histories that were long hidden, and inseparably entwined, in the landscape of central Australia. Through his policing, his photography and newspaper articles, his collections of central Australian landscapes and histories, and his ceaseless determination to emulate explorers like John McDouall Stuart and Cecil Madigan, he was a key figure in the violent history we'd erased from national memory and, at the same time, a contributor to the powerful myths of the center we've invented since.

Like many of those who document history, he also curated the images of the past he left behind. Before I left Brisbane on that second visit in 2019, Susan and Ian Golledge showed me a photograph of McKinnon. It was Susan's favorite. Her father was camped near Barrow Creek, about 175 miles north of Alice Springs, playing the violin by firelight and sitting on a wooden Shell motor oil box that I'd seen in Susan's garage. The photograph was obviously staged but unlike any other image I'd seen of him.

Using his camera's self-timer, McKinnon had choreographed the scene. The shutter needed to stay open for several seconds to record the image. He sits still on the old oil box, bathed in the ambient light of the campfire, imitating movement but not really playing, lest his upper body appear blurred. His crossed legs, his slightly tilted head, and the carefully positioned props—the sharply focused music stand, his teacup, the tent, and the large branch in the foreground—lend the photograph a distinctly romantic air.

True to form, McKinnon provided the context on the back of the photograph. "On my last camel patrol, in 1941. The first and only time that I carried the violin. Was playing it one evening—moved on to hymns, when my trackers, 'Police Paddy' and 'Carbine,' started singing. Called them over from their fire, and they said they had learned them at Hermannsburg. So we had a bush concert."

Almost fifty years later, as he looked back on this luminous moment in his life, McKinnon was exultant: "Oh, that was enjoyable."

McKinnon had cornered Yokununna in the darkness of a cave inside Uluru. For Yokununna, looking out toward the entrance of the cave, there was one slowly widening shaft of light that led to the place where McKinnon waited with his pistol poised. There was no chance of escape. Thinking of Yokununna's skull filed away in the museum's collection of human remains, and the documents I'd uncovered in McKinnon's basement in a Brisbane garage, it seemed to me that the events at Uluru in 1934 were still shrouded in the darkness in which they'd begun.

Although the world McKinnon inhabited in central Australia in the 1930s was less than a century ago, much of it seemed lost to view—another time and historical context, one that was both recognizable and foreign. I found it difficult to comprehend the pervasive culture of violence: the punching, whipping, kicking, bashing, and rifle fire that were such a common part of McKinnon's policing on his early patrols; the sound of his and his trackers' raised voices as they extracted confessions from their charges, their private conversation and silences, and the racial borders between them that they knew instinctively never to cross. This was a world in which white station owners never traveled unarmed and always slept with a revolver close to hand, a world in which every white male was a de facto policeman and where anger and frustration could easily spill over into violence, as it did at Uluru, when, after days of chasing his quarry across the desert sands, McKinnon fired into a cave to hit a defenseless man.

McKinnon was no stranger to bullet wounds himself. On March 3, 1925, as a young policeman in New South Wales, he nearly lost his life when a rifle he was cleaning accidentally discharged. The ".22

Bill McKinnon, near Barrow Creek, 1941

short caliber bullet" entered his head and shattered into thirteen pieces, one of which lodged "in the matter surrounding [his] brain" and damaged his left optic nerve, leaving his vision permanently impaired. After three weeks' treatment in Sydney Hospital—hot baths and "one dose of castor oil"—he was left with fragments embedded in his skull for the rest of his life.

Other aspects of his life that I saw in those documents from his daughter's garage—and traces of his personality—were more familiar to me. In McKinnon, I recognized some of the men I'd grown up with in the western suburbs of Sydney in the 1960s and '70s. The tough exterior; the dry, biting humor; the unyielding, granitic discipline; the fierce loyalty to his mates and his white Australian tribe. He was relentless in carrying out what he saw as his duty, even when it led him into brutality and worse. Yet to heap responsibility for what happened at Uluru in 1934 onto McKinnon's shoulders alone is to fail to understand the moral and political complexities of the time and place in which he lived.

McKinnon enforced a legal system that was brutally and swiftly imposed on the lands and peoples of central Australia, just as it had been imposed on every square mile of the Australian continent since colonization began—without the consent of its Indigenous owners. In seeking to uphold what he saw as the law, he served a system that asserted the power and right of the invaders to take land at will; a system that brought thousands of cattle, erected fences and borders, pushed Aboriginal people off their Country, created reserves that suited whitefellas' economic designs, exploited Aboriginal labor, and created new myths of possession: bruised, laconic tales of bittersweet conquest, which cast the country as the hard-won property of a handful of white men.

Bill McKinnon was one such man. As he insisted when he retired from the Northern Territory Police, "There are many loyal and sensible people in the Territory who still believe in people obeying the laws of the land, and also feel that laws are made by parliament to be enforced by parliament." Yet it was precisely the laws of the land—prescribed by legislation and put into effect by government officials, police, courts, judges, and prisons—that subverted Indigenous law and culture. McKinnon was the dogged soldier on the front line of an entire structure that sanctioned invasion and dispossession. The injustice of what took place at Uluru in 1934 was one graphic example of a much larger injustice perpetrated against the Aboriginal people of Australia that continues to this day. The Anangu, of course, know this history better than anyone, as Sammy Wilson told Jen Cowley in 2018:

> It's still happening, that divide between traditional law and white law. . . . Once the fences were built, the Anangu would still go and walk their country, but the whitefellas would say, "Hey, what are you doing here? This is my land." And the Anangu didn't understand that the fences they'd put up meant it was no longer their land, according to the whitefella way. . . . It's still a shock . . . that this is our country but because they put the fences up it's now their country.

As I prepared to return to Uluru, I kept thinking about Sammy's ongoing shock regarding the Anangu's dispossession: a shock that non-Indigenous Australians have yet to comprehend. Although they inhabit the same continent, they belong to a different historical experience. Bill McKinnon was nominated for an Order of Australia in 1995 by Brian Bennett, local historian of the Northern Territory Police, who described him as a "living national treasure." This stands in contrast to the Anangu's memory of the same man, the policeman who mercilessly killed Yokununna and who later separated children from their mothers—two histories divided by a vast chasm.

At Uluru, John Carty and I would arrive with the heavy news that Yokununna's skull was in the South Australian Museum. Because his killing was a seminal moment for the Anangu in the wake of European invasion, and the place where it occurred was now seen as the spiritual heart of the continent, the repatriation of Yokununna's remains was at once of family, community, Territory, and national significance. I was acutely aware that the Anangu's telling of this history differed substantially from the history I've written here. When Sammy Wilson told the story of the shooting, he would not mention McKinnon's name, the circumstances under which he had arrested Yokununna, or the precise location of the shooting. Nor, of course, have the Anangu chosen to make any mention of the events of 1934 in the interpretative panels that grace Uluru today.

Would Sammy welcome the disclosure of all the details surrounding the shooting near Mutitjulu Waterhole? In telling the story of the shooting, he was naturally bound by Anangu law. Would he ask that I, too, respect that law and refrain from revealing that the Dreaming battle between Kuniya and Liru had occurred in the very same place that McKinnon shot Yokununna?

And what of the other side of the story? How would McKinnon's family react when I returned to Brisbane and explained the full import of the book? Would they try to bar publication of some of the details I'd found among McKinnon's papers in their garage? As I left the family garage on my second visit to Brisbane, McKinnon's grandson Ian turned toward me and said firmly: "We need more Aboriginal history."

Six months later, I met Ian's brother Matt Golledge, Susan's youngest son, at a café on Eagle Street in the center of Brisbane. He was warm and appreciative of the opportunity to discuss the book. We sat at an outside table in the midday heat, talking for what seemed like minutes but was well over two hours.

Although I'd imagined that the family knew something of McKinnon's experience in central Australia, Matt recalled only a few anecdotes he'd been told as a child. When I asked him what he knew about the events at Uluru in 1934, he shook his head. "Nothing," he said, shrugging his shoulders. "We didn't read all the stuff that Granddad left in the garage." I had been in this situation once or twice before—the historian who arrives on a family's doorstep with knowledge of their relative gleaned from combing the archives, most of which is entirely unknown to them—but I'd never had to relate a story such as this. Haltingly, I began to tell Matt something of his grandfather's life and work in central Australia.

When I came to the shooting at Uluru, he listened attentively, nodding occasionally, sometimes with eyebrows raised, especially as I described how I'd found the original journal in the garage that proved McKinnon was lying to the Commonwealth Board of Inquiry. "The smoking gun," he said pointedly.

As we continued to talk, it became clear that I'd arrived at a difficult time. Matt told me of the challenges his family had faced managing Susan's care as her dementia advanced. I had come thinking that I would do most of the talking, but I left having spent as much time listening—reminding me again of how much I was asking of him. "I've got all this going on," he said, "and now you come here to tell me this. What's next?" His main concern, he explained, was "Mum." He was worried that in granting me access to McKinnon's papers in her garage, Susan would feel she had undermined or even betrayed her father, whom she had always idolized and loved. And all this at the end of her life.

It was an uncomfortable truth. The book—or news of it, for Susan already found it difficult to read for more than a few minutes—could

Reggie Uluru, flanked by fellow elders Nellie Patterson and Yuka Trigger, November 2019

easily prove unsettling for her or other members of the family. Regardless of what they thought of my intentions, or the way I had approached the story, they still had to deal with the book's fallout in a way that no other reader would have to do. I wondered if this would be the moment when Matt's reservations would spill over into resistance.

After hearing everything I had to tell him about his grandfather's life, he leaned back slightly in his chair, arms outstretched. "I can see the bigger historical perspective," he said. "All of the family, Mum included, are on board for reconciliation. We wouldn't want anything else."

9

STATEMENT FROM
THE LIVING HEART

In early November 2019, just before my last visit to Brisbane and only weeks after the Uluru climb was officially closed, Reggie Uluru, flanked by fellow elders Nellie Patterson and Yuka Trigger, held up the last chain removed from the rock's summit in triumph. The safety chain that had marched up Uluru as an aid to climbers since the early 1960s was a potent symbol for all Anangu, not only of whitefellas' disregard for their law but of the chains that had shackled their lives: fences and borders, neck chains and handcuffs, shootings and massacres, and countless ordinances and policies imposed without their consent. As helicopters took away the last sections of the chain, stonemasons dismantled the cairn begun by William Gosse in 1873 and photographed by Bill McKinnon when he climbed the rock in 1932. What McKinnon and so many other white Australians had imagined as the first steps in the discovery of central Australia had become little more than an eyeblink in Uluru's history.

In the months before the climb closed, the number of tourists arriving at the rock rose sharply. Hotels and camping grounds were booked out. With nowhere else to go, some visitors set up camp illegally by the roadside, leaving their rubbish behind as they departed, usually after an average stay of no more than forty-eight hours. The "caterpillar" trail of four-wheel drives and caravans crawled toward the car park at the base of the rock, while hundreds of cars were left parked on either side of the road, their occupants deciding to walk the final kilometer to their destination. As the steady line of climbers ascended Uluru, they followed the path worn into the rock's surface by the millions who'd preceded them. Among them were Drew Martin and his two daughters, descendants of Charles Mountford. Martin believed that most climbers were there "out of some sort of respect for Aboriginal culture." Others saw their presence as an assertion of their national identity: "We're Aussies, so we've come to climb the rock." Many had rushed to tick the climb off their "bucket list." The phrase said much about the gulf between the Anangu's understanding of Uluru—McKinnon himself had noted how they chose not to climb the rock "for tribal reasons"—and that of the tourists eager to take their trophy "selfie" on the summit. The struggle to close the climb had been long and difficult.

In May 1966, Bill and Doreen Hunt, who led groups on Sundowner Coaches bus tours to Uluru, decided to place a notebook and pen at the top of the rock. As the couple later explained, "The idea . . . originated [with] one of our clients, Ray Hopkins of Liverpool, Sydney," who on his second bus trip to Uluru "brought the first book and steel case and mounted" them on top of the rock. It was a textual version of the small pile of stones left by Gosse a century earlier. The Hunts hoped that future climbers, whom they described as "brave types," might leave behind their names and addresses and perhaps a comment reflecting on their experience. Even before the first climber's name had been recorded, the Hunts were well aware of the historical value of their idea, instructing the ranger, Bob Gregory, to "keep" each book, as it filled with the names and reflections of visitors from Australia and overseas, "for posterity." The opening page

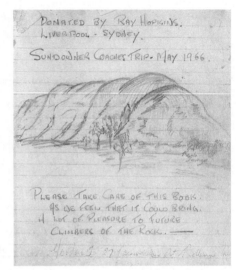

"Ayer's Rock" Climbers Registry,
May 1966

of their first book—simply illustrated with a pencil sketch, its lined pages stained and fingerprinted with a thin film of red dust—evokes something of the magnetic attraction the rock held for them and so many of their fellow travelers.

In books like this over the next twenty years, climbers registered their names and thoughts when they had completed the steep one-mile trek to the top of the rock. Looking at the comments that were left behind—"Once is enough," "Never again," "Maybe next time in a helicopter, stubby and all," "Where in hell is the bloody coke machine and letter box?"—what's striking is their irreverence and the almost complete absence of any mention of Indigenous culture. As one climber wrote baldly in 1984: "a rock is only a rock." A few felt "closer to [their] God" once they'd finally completed the arduous trek to the top. Others were inspired to write poems: "red monarch towering over the desert sands . . . brief is our triumph, for we know [it's] true that we'll soon vanish from this earth."

But the overwhelming majority of climbers simply signed their name and their place and country of origin, occasionally leaving a brief reflection: "11.3.1984, Peter Severin, Curtin Springs Station"; "Bill McKinnon, Buderim Q. (first climbed in Feb. 1932, much harder now)."

McKinnon's signature—a tiny, cursive script—was surrounded by others from German, Swiss, and Finnish tourists, who complained of the ferocious heat. One month after he stood on the summit, as the Anangu's demands for land rights at Uluru reached fever pitch, it became possible to find comments such as this: "I hope the Aboriginals don't lose their whole rock."

In 1986, the climbing registers that had remained at the top of the rock for twenty years were removed. Anangu elders, having at last won the right to manage the park in conjunction with the National Parks and Wildlife Service, decided not to disallow the climb because they knew "how much it meant to whitefellas." At the same time, they made it clear that they "were not very happy about it." Although they had little choice but to leave the safety chain in place after several climbers suffered injuries and fatalities—almost forty people died climbing the rock since records began in 1950—the decision to remove the registers helped to undermine the triumphant imagery of the ascent. However, I CLIMBED ULURU certificates, badges, and T-shirts had long been sold to tourists and could still be purchased in 2019.

As Uluru gained World Heritage status in 1987, and in 1994 became "the second national park in the world" to be listed by UNESCO as a "cultural landscape," calls to end the climb become impossible to ignore. More and more "ants," or *minga* (the Pitjantjatjara word for tourists), arrived every year, and by the time the mud-brick Cultural Centre opened in 1995, the Anangu had erected signs requesting that tourists not climb out of respect for their culture. Inside, visitors now had the opportunity to sign the "I did not climb Uluru" register. In the space of three decades, tourists had gone from proudly proclaiming their conquest of the rock to conveying their solidarity with Anangu elders.

Taking time to comb through the pages of these latter-day registers when I visited Uluru, I was immediately struck by the radical difference in content and tone compared to the comments left in the climbing registers three decades earlier. Aside from the most common refrain—visitors claiming that they decided not to climb Uluru out of *respect* for Anangu culture—it was their reflections on the importance of land and its spiritual significance that stood out.

> "I am not religious but [visiting Uluru] was the first time I had felt this powerful pull to the land";
> "I'm fascinated by a culture that tries to live as one with land and nature";
> "I'm amazed by the truth and honesty in your way of living";
> "I felt a powerful spiritual connection";
> "Modern cultures have lost their sense of belonging to the universe";
> "We have detached ourselves from nature";
> "Close the walk up Uluru, it's encouraging people to be complete cultural jerks."

The words used repeatedly by those who had taken the trouble to sign—"healing," "spiritual," "enchanting," "holy," "sacred," "moving," "awe-inspiring," "overwhelming," "beyond description," and "serenity"—spoke not only to Australians' newfound respect for Indigenous culture and the transformation of Uluru into a spiritual center, but also to the nostalgia of many for a simpler, preindustrial world, embedded in place and community. Superficially, the aura of Uluru appears as an antidote to problems plaguing contemporary societies across the globe. Uluru's mystique—its sacred status—is both a belated recognition of Anangu civilization and a reminder of what modern, secular societies have lost or struggle to find: belonging, spirituality, singular tradition, and connection with the natural world. In this pursuit of an almost religious connection to place, ironies abound.

Non-Aboriginal visitors come annually in their hundreds of thousands to Uluru to feel "connected" to the land and the continent's ancient Indigenous heritage, the very same heritage that Australian society had for so long sought to eradicate. Creation stories that were once dismissed as little more than superstition are now widely recognized as forming part of a nationwide "web of mythologies." At Uluru, nearly all the conventional ways of thinking about the relationship between Indigenous people and their colonizers have been inverted. A people who were seen purely in pejorative terms now stand proudly as the valued custodians of environmental and cultural knowledge. Tjukurpa, "the foundation of Anangu life and society," is presented as a "living" exemplar, a way forward rather than a relic of the past. The very cultures from which we wished for so long to be free, we now long to embrace.

Not far away, in the shadow of Uluru, stands the community of Mutitjulu, the catalyst for the Howard government's 2007 intervention into Aboriginal communities in the Northern Territory, after a government report documented alarming levels of sexual abuse and domestic violence. Here, as author Nicolas Rothwell found in 2013, seventeen service providers fought "for control of fewer than 300 souls." In the midst of constantly expanding government control of their lives, the community confronted yet another wave of "recolonisation." "How do you restore voice and power to people whom you have lured into dependency?" Rothwell asked, a people "whose past and future obsess the intelligentsia and opinion-formers, yet whose present circumstances are too disquieting to keep in view?" In 2015, on the thirtieth anniversary of the handback of Uluru, Sammy Wilson, chair of the board of Uluru–Kata Tjuta National Park, claimed that tourism at the rock was "sucking everything like a vacuum cleaner from Anangu toward the resort." Anangu people, he claimed, "were missing out."

When Wilson announced the closure of the climb in October 2017, a decision taken after years of deliberation and because the overwhelming majority of visitors chose to respect Anangu law by not climbing the rock, he reminded visitors that Uluru was not "Disneyland" and explained why the closure had finally become necessary.

> Whitefellas see the land in economic terms, where Anangu see it as Tjukurpa . . . money is transient . . . Tjukurpa is everlasting. . . . Over the years Anangu have felt a sense of intimidation, as if someone is holding a gun to our heads to keep [the climb] open. Please don't hold us to ransom. . . . Closing the climb is . . . a cause for celebration . . . let's close it together.

The environmental impact of the climb—erosion; memorials to dead climbers; feces, urine, and toilet paper scattered across the rock's surface; litter and runoff washing into water holes—mirrored the larger impact of "settlement" on central Australia, in which "40 percent of native species . . . are either extinct or locally extinct." Many that remain are rare and endangered. Introduced species—such as the notorious buffel grass, imported from South Africa in the late 1880s, and feral populations of camels, cattle, cats, horses, donkeys, and foxes—have denuded soil and vegetation. Across the region, enormous environmental challenges confront government, private enterprise, and national parks. Despite the closure of the climb, many tourists lack the time and inclination to understand the broader impact of their numbers on the rock and the surrounding country.

Uluru, 2013

Like the Leyland Brothers' grotesque "Ayers Rock Roadhouse" on the Pacific Highway north of Newcastle, which opened in 1990 (and burned down in 2018), complete with fake rock, amusement rides, and imitation "bush camps," the threat of a Disneyland theme park remains.

Today, tourists can experience the rock at sunset with canapés and chilled sparkling wine followed by a "bush tucker inspired buffet . . . under the stars," serenaded by the didgeridoo. Uluru tours offer everything from yoga, meditation, and dance workshops to New Age "soul therapy" sessions, "energetic healing," evenings of "chant and contemplation," and "cosmic consciousness" events that guarantee a "shared spiritual experience" as participants "humbly connect to the rainbow serpent." "Car sunset" and "bus sunset" car parks provide ideal vantage points for tourists to photograph the rock; light installations "enhance" the natural landscape to entertain visitors at night, and "SkyShip Uluru," a gargantuan blimp balloon, rises five hundred feet above ground level to give them an aerial view of the rock. But not even this heady amalgam of genuine cross-cultural tourism, kitsch, and vulgar commercialism can destroy the truth and integrity of the Anangu's message. Most visitors come to learn. They take part in "Aboriginal experience" tours, allowing them to "connect and share experiences with the world's oldest living culture." Guides lead "campfire stories," "traditional bush skill" sessions, and Uluru teaching walks.

The more lasting evidence of Uluru's newfound esteem in the national imagination is undeniable. In 1988, when the government funded an advertising campaign to promote the bicentenary of British settlement in Australia, it used the rock as a visual backdrop for a choir of stranded celebrities belting out the theme of the year's festivities: "Celebration of a Nation." In 2000, the Sydney Olympic torch began its journey with a circuit around the base of Uluru, while the design of the National Museum of Australia, opened in 2001, incorporated the so-called Uluru line, ending in a "curled concrete ramp that, conceptually, continues northwest to Uluru."

Memorialized in advertising, art, film, and music—including works by popular Australian composers as diverse as Ross Edwards ("Laughing Rock"), Peter Sculthorpe ("Into the Dreaming"), Katia Beaugeais ("First Light at Uluru"), Goanna ("Solid Rock"), and Midnight Oil ("The Dead Heart")—Uluru had become *the* place, perhaps more than any other, where Australia's Indigenous and non-Indigenous histories merge. Its significance had shifted not only for non-Indigenous Australians, but also for Indigenous people living in other parts of the country. Stephen Page, artistic director of the Bangarra Dance Theatre, has spoken of the importance of Uluru to his artistic vision, ever since he first encountered it on a cultural exchange trip as an eighteen-year-old dance student from southeast Queensland. Seeing it, he said, "changed my perspective about the land and how it's so connected to our people . . . the greatness of it . . . the fullness of it . . . the rock is almost like a north-south-east-west songlines connection to many stories around the country . . . we're threaded [through] storytelling . . . to that wonder." No more graphic example can be found of Uluru as a meeting place for Australia's histories than the National Constitutional Convention being held there in 2017. Yet not even this moment was free from the specter of Bill McKinnon's actions in 1934.

After extensive nationwide consultation, Indigenous leaders traveled from all around the country to Uluru, where they agreed on the way forward for constitutional reform. The Uluru Statement from the Heart, which called for a constitutionally enshrined Indigenous advisory body (the Voice) and the establishment of a Makarrata Commission to supervise treaties and truth-telling on a national scale, was released at Uluru in May 2017. As Uluru's national park general manager, Michael Misso, noted, the site was no accident. The evidence for Uluru's status as "the spiritual center of the nation," he said, was clear from the decision to hold the convention there in the first place. "They didn't choose Canberra," he remarked pointedly. Convention delegate and Yolngu elder Galarrwuy Yunupingu stressed that Aboriginal and Torres Strait Islander peoples were linked "throughout the country by songlines and kinship" and were honored to be "in the presence of the greatest rock of all, Uluru, our heart and the heart of our nation." His brother Dhayirra hoped that the decision to announce the Statement from the Heart at the foot of such an "iconic site" would make it easier for "the *balanda* [whitefellas] to understand."

By issuing the statement's three demands—"Voice, Treaty and Truth"—at Uluru, not only did the nation's Indigenous leaders confirm it as the country's spiritual and emotional "center"; they also married Uluru and its myriad associations for black and white alike with poetic constitutional language, the kind of language that is so glaringly absent from the Australian constitution. Uluru now named a sacred text as well as a sacred place. In this potentially nation-defining moment, it became what Canberra had never been: the spiritual center of the Commonwealth.

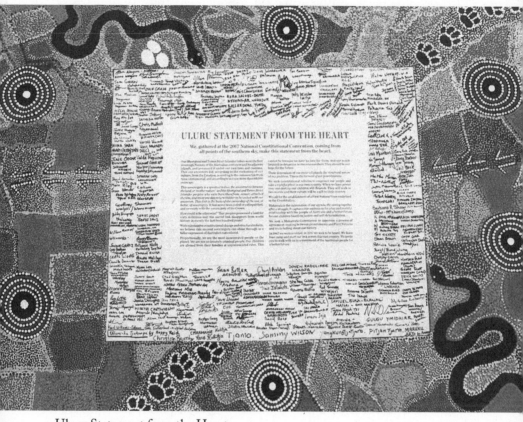

Uluru Statement from the Heart

Like earlier calls for Indigenous rights, such as the 1963 Yirrkala bark petitions and the Barunga Statement presented to Prime Minister Bob Hawke in 1988, the Uluru Statement from the Heart, as journalist Stephen Fitzpatrick noted, arrived wrapped in art, dance, and song. Australians were being asked to embrace not only the text of the document but an entire body of Indigenous knowledge. At Uluru, "clan leaders performed a dance about the fire, or *gurtha*, that links the Yolngu people of Northeast Arnhem Land with the Anangu." The statement, written on canvas, was accompanied by the signatures of more than 250 delegates from more than one hundred First Nations.

The artwork that surrounds the text was painted by senior Maruku artist and Uluru traditional owner Rene Kulitja, with fellow Mutitjulu artists Christine Brumby, Charmaine Kulitja, and Happy Reid. Rene explained how the "painting shows all the stories of Uluru and the statement is placed at the center where the power resides." It depicts two of the most significant creation stories at Uluru, the story of the Mala people and the story of Kuniya, the woman python with eggs, who battles Liru, the poisonous snake from the southwest, in a fight to the death at Mutitjulu Waterhole.

The Anangu's public account of the battle between Kuniya and Liru ends with Liru's death. As he dies, Liru drops his shield, which can be seen today as the large boulder near Mutitjulu Waterhole, where "Kuniya herself remains as a sinuous black line on the eastern wall." In one rock shelter at Mutitjulu, "a row of concentric circles represents the eggs of the *kuniya* python."

During the 1935 board of inquiry into Yokununna's death, McKinnon was asked to identify the precise place where the shooting had occurred. He led the members of the board to the entrance of the cave's outer cavern, and even crouched down to demonstrate the position from which he had fired into the inner cavern. Each step of his simulation was photographed—"Maggie Springs," "entrance to outer cavern," "position from which Constable McKinnon fired the fatal shot into the inner cavern"—the photos eventually appearing in the board's final report. One of the photos, "scene of shooting" (page 198, top right), is taken from a distance and marked with a black arrow, possibly drawn by McKinnon himself. It shows the precise place where he claimed to have fired at Yokununna.

The triangular slab of broken rock where the arrow's line ends is the shield of Liru, behind which is the entrance to the cave where McKinnon stood with his pistol. McKinnon shot Yokununna on the very same battleground where the fight between Kuniya and Liru took place.

Uluru's creation story and the frontier murder that defined the killing times for the Anangu more than any other event in the twentieth century took place at the same sacred site. The Uluru Statement from the Heart, which calls for "truth-telling" about Australia's history, is literally enfolded in a painting that speaks from the very place where the truth of the Anangu's possession of Country was so violently denied. And of course, Anangu elder and Uluru custodian Sammy Wilson, the man who gave final permission for the name "Uluru" to be used in the title of the statement, is personally linked to the events of 1934 through his grandfather, Paddy. The Uluru family believe that Paddy's father met William Gosse near Mutitjulu Waterhole in 1873. The whitefella lineage of "discoverers," "pioneers," station owners, police, scientists, missionaries, humanitarians, and murderers is threaded through the family history of Uluru's custodians like barbed wire.

The lines of history have continued to cross in this one place in surprising ways. When members of the British royal family or other dignitaries visited Uluru in the late twentieth century, they were led to Mutitjulu Waterhole on official tours. Reggie and Cassidy Uluru danced for them. The interweaving of the stories at the water hole— Uluru's ancient songlines, "a kind of scripture" that expresses the

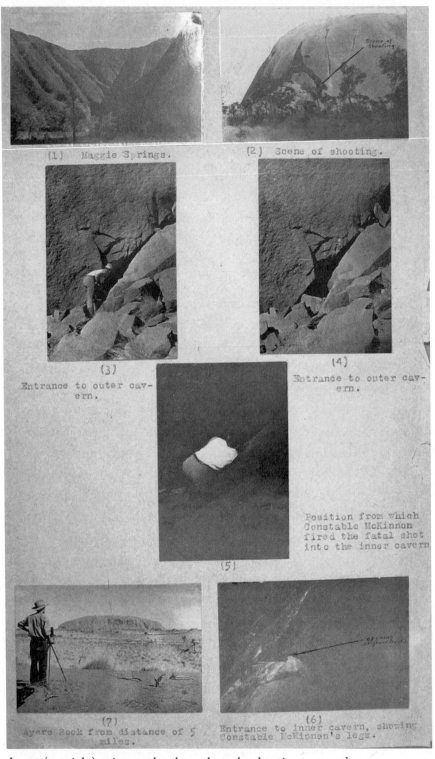

(1)   Maggie Springs.

(2)   Scene of shooting.

(3)

Entrance to outer cavern.

(4)

Entrance to outer cavern.

Position from which Constable McKinnon fired the fatal shot into the inner cavern

(5)

(7)

Ayers Rock from distance of 5 miles.

(6)

Entrance to inner cavern, showing Constable McKinnon's legs.

Arrow (top right) points to the place where the shooting occurred

Anangu's relationship to Country as inalienable law, and the pioneer legends of Europeans in central Australia—is almost too intricate and vast to hold in one field of vision. As author Barry Hill reflected, if we could grasp this heady mix of cultural knowledge and "pilgrims' tales" at Uluru, we would come close to the "song of the center."

The extraordinary coalescence of these histories at Mutitjulu Waterhole provides a powerfully charged site for *makarrata*—"coming together after a struggle." The "sovereignty" of Indigenous Australians—immutable and inextinguishable—is visible at Uluru as it is at few other places in the continent. And it is here that Indigenous relations with Commonwealth and Territory governments are negotiated on a daily basis. The Mutitjulu community near Uluru has struggled to realize the high hopes for its future held after the handback in 1985—yet another reason Australia's First Nations people have demanded a constitutionally enshrined Voice to Parliament. After more than 230 years, they want a say in the creation of the laws that govern their lives. Even if this goal is realized, the sovereignty of the Crown indisputably remains ascendant. Australians have yet to grasp the fact that the core rationale for an Australian republic is not only the severance of our relationship with the Crown, but also the recognition of the Indigenous sovereignty that existed long before the Crown's representatives arrived.

Summing up his experience in central Australia in the 1930s, Cecil Madigan's grim conclusion was that "the whole question" of relations between Aboriginal people and white Australians could be "brought down to this simple alternative: either the settler occupies the country and the native, even if treated with the utmost humanity, vanishes before the advance of a civilization that is utterly beyond him, or else the country is left untouched, in which alone lies the salvation of the native. The European and the Australian Aboriginal cannot exist together." After nearly a century of oppression since his verdict—killings; racist laws; countless mistaken attempts to

View from Kulpi Mutitjulu, the "family" cave

extinguish, assimilate, and manage Aboriginal people on the part of white Australians; and the long fight for justice, adaptation, and survival led by Indigenous Australians and their collaborators—Madigan has been shown to be a false prophet. As Rene Kulitja remarked when she was asked about her painting that enfolds the Uluru Statement: "I think a lot about the two worlds that we live in now—the non-Anangu world, the whitefella world, the mainstream world, and the Anangu cultural world. I think about how to work within both worlds, how to bring them together so we're supporting each other with strong knowledge about both worlds." The history of relations between the Anangu and their usurpers has demonstrated that it *is* possible for white and black Australians to live together. Yet it also reveals how selective our embrace of Uluru has been. The much-vaunted "spiritual center" of Australia is inseparable from the nation's foundational violence. Australia may have belatedly discovered the center, but it has only recognized one part of the truth of Uluru.

10

DESERT OAK NO. 1

I n 1935 John Cleland and the board traveled from Uluru to Alice Springs and then returned to Adelaide with Yokununna's remains, but where were they now? James Warden published one of the first scholarly articles on the shooting at Uluru and the board of inquiry in 2002. Before I first visited Susan in Brisbane in 2019, he reminded me to check whether Yokununna's remains had been deposited in museum collections. Around the same time, I came across a recollection of McKinnon's, in which he bluntly stated what had happened: "The remains of Yokununna [were] removed for conveyance to Adelaide Museum where I understand they are still down in the basement." I emailed the two most likely possibilities: the University of Adelaide, where Cleland had worked, and the South Australian Museum. There was no immediate response.

Museum official Professor John Carty and I had planned to meet Uluru community leader Sammy Wilson in late March 2020—but the COVID-19 pandemic canceled those plans. All nonessential domestic travel was banned. Indigenous communities, who were more vulnerable than most given the prevalence of preexisting health conditions among their populations, moved swiftly to deny access to outsiders, while the Northern Territory government closed its borders.

I emailed Sammy and his partner, Kathy Tozer, asking if I could speak to them by phone or video link. Several weeks later, I heard from Kathy. John Carty and I had already agreed that if an opportunity arose to speak on the phone, I would tell Sammy and Kathy the news. We would then arrange an online meeting to discuss arrangements for the repatriation of Yokununna's remains.

Kathy explained that Sammy was extremely busy dealing with the threat the virus posed to the Anangu. Could I possibly tell her what I wanted to speak to him about? I began to do so slowly, but before I could get very far she interrupted me. "Wait," she said. "Sammy's in the next room. I'll get him." As I revealed the information—yes, Yokununna's skull was with the museum, and Bill McKinnon had lived well into his nineties and returned to Uluru as an old man—I could feel their astonishment down the line.

Kathy, who is fluent in Pitjantjatjara, translated for Sammy as I talked. Although he spoke English, this story was so important that it had to be returned to him in his own language. I paused after every sentence and listened as she told it to Sammy, who interjected, sometimes in English, sometimes in Pitjantjatjara. As I heard the story narrated in Yokununna's language, I felt that this was the first step in bringing him home.

Yokununna's life story could only truly be understood through his own people's telling of it in Country. Although I knew little of him from documentary sources, which had reduced him to nothing more than an "escaped prisoner," those same sources contained details that McKinnon had long tried to suppress. When I explained to Kathy and Sammy that I'd also made contact with McKinnon's family and that I'd found crucial evidence relating to the killing in his daughter's garage, the whole import of the revelations became clear. Kathy said that Sammy was so moved he was speechless.

The following year, in July, during the (Southern Hemisphere) winter of 2020, when I'd almost given up hope of reaching Uluru, the first wave of COVID-19 had subsided and the Northern Territory's borders were reopened. In early August, with some trepidation, tourists were allowed to visit Uluru. Although John Carty was unable to accompany me, I immediately arranged to fly from Canberra to Alice Springs and drive the 275 miles to the rock. Stopping for fuel at Curtin Springs Roadhouse on the way, I walked into the bar and noticed a large, framed black-and-white photograph hanging over the doorway. Taken in 1986, it showed McKinnon and his second wife, Olga, standing proudly with the station owner, Peter Severin. Severin, aged ninety-two, whom I'd tried unsuccessfully to interview after several approaches some months earlier, was still living on Curtin Springs Station. I decided not to press the matter and drove on to Uluru.

Seven years after my first encounter with it, the rock was no less breathtaking. Only this time I saw it with the full knowledge of what had happened there in 1934. Uluru now seemed to contain not only the secrets and legends of the Anangu, but the truth of white Australia's centuries-long determination to obliterate Indigenous culture as well.

At 10 a.m. on Wednesday, August 12, I drove from Yulara to Mutitjulu Waterhole. It was a clear, windless morning, the sky cobalt blue, the green leaves of the bloodwoods and the white bark of the river red gums luminous against the red hulk of the rock. Up close, the vastness of Uluru was lost. At the water hole, the arms of the rock enfolded me. It was easy to see why so many visitors over the years had felt that this place offered shelter and sustenance. It's an intimate, cloistered space. Even when bone dry, the dark, snakelike traces of the water falling down the rock seem reassuring.

After all this time, it was an honor to meet Paddy Uluru's sons, Reggie and Cassidy—resplendent in their brightly banded cowboy hats and star-studded belts—and Sammy, his firstborn grandson, together with Kathy Tozer. Cassidy was eager to tell me about the water hole and its cultural importance, especially Kulpi Mutitjulu, the "family" cave, where his father had painted as a boy. Native figs like those that Strehlow observed in 1935 could still be seen growing nearby. He explained how the concentric circles visible on the roof of the cave represented a water hole, and he drew my attention to a painting of the honey grevillea.

"We tell whitefellas a few things," said Cassidy, smiling, "but not everything." As we moved on to discuss the story of the shooting, I took out my phone and passed round the photographs taken during the board of inquiry, one of which showed an arrow pointing to the base of the shield of Liru, where Yokununna was killed, and another

Sammy Wilson, Cassidy Uluru, and Reggie Uluru

of McKinnon, crouching in front of the entrance to the cave where he had fired at Yokununna.

As soon as Sammy saw the photographs, he took off, scampering up the rock in his thongs and old peaked cap. "Let's go and find it," he said excitedly. I followed him without thinking. If I was going to break a limb, I couldn't think of a better reason than climbing up the huge boulders that were piled at the foot of the rock. The hike up to the shield of Liru was only a little over forty feet (exactly as McKinnon had said), but in thirty-degree heat (eighty-six degrees Fahrenheit), it felt like twice the distance. Sammy, who told me how he'd scaled these same rocks as a boy, seemed to retrieve his boyish enthusiasm the farther we climbed. Stopping now and then to look at my phone, he compared two or three crevices unsuccessfully to the photograph of McKinnon standing outside the cave entrance. Not until we stood behind the shield of Liru, after searching for half an hour, did Sammy finally recognize the spot: "Look!" he exclaimed, pointing to a small opening in the rock. "Here it is."

Some of the rocks had moved over the years, and the entrance to the cave had become smaller, but the telltale sign—a triangular cutting in the rock that can be seen in the photo on page 208—left no doubt. Digital technology and cultural knowledge combined forces. Sammy asked me to take his photograph as he stood pointing to the opening in the rock.

Standing there with him, I thought of the ear-splitting echo of gunfire that must have terrified the four men who had sought refuge at Uluru in 1934. On-site, Yokununna's death seemed even more unjust, horrifying, and unnecessary, the defenseless man's vulnerability even more obvious.

Sammy was proud to have personally identified the spot where his granduncle had lost his life eighty-six years earlier. As we descended, he showed me a "spear bush." Paddy Uluru had taught him how to

Sammy Wilson pointing at the spot where Yokununna was killed

make spears when he was a boy—"We still make them today," he said. Then he started to tell me the story of Kuniya and Liru in the most animated fashion. "What do you see?" he asked me directly, pointing to the "family cave," which was just below the shield of Liru, where we had stood only a few minutes earlier. Before I could reply, he called out: "It's an eye, can't you see? It's Kuniya herself. She's there."

He walked over to the old bloodwood behind us and showed me where the wood had been taken to make a shield many years ago. We had found the place where Yokununna was killed, but for Sammy, that event, as important as it was, would never be allowed to overshadow the larger significance of the site. Everything around him—the trees and shrubs, the paintings on the cave walls, the jumble of boulders at Liru's feet, the scars on the face of the rock, and the water hole itself—was alive. Past and present were one. Before we left the water hole, he pointed again to Kuniya's face, encased in the rock. "You have to understand," he implored. "For us, it's like a sacred statue."

The cathedral-like images of Uluru that had dominated Europeans' first impressions of the rock had returned but were now used by the Anangu to convey the significance of their sacred sites to visitors. Twenty-four hours later, back in Alice Springs, I received a text from Kathy Tozer. "Sammy's been very inspired and he is traveling to Areyonga [en route to Alice Springs] as I text. He's found out the descendants of Paddy's brother [Yokununna], who was apparently also called Kurkara (desert oak) No. 1."

Two weeks later, a second text arrived. "Hello Mark, Sammy was very keen for you to get these photos he took at Areyonga. The older man with Sammy is Abraham Poulson, who is the grandson of Yokununna/Kurkara through his younger brother known as Kurkara malatja ('desert oak the latter' or Kurkara No. 2). The younger man

Paddy Uluru's and Yokununna's grandsons and great-grandsons. In the first photograph, Sammy Wilson (left) with Abraham Poulson (right); in the second photograph, Sammy's son, Ken (left), with Abraham Poulson's son, Stefan (right)

on the right is Abraham's son, Stefan, with Sammy's own son, Ken, on the left."

Desert oaks stand in the sand dunes around Uluru—slender and upright in their juvenile form, their foliage prickly, their bark thick, their taproots anchored deep in the red earth—resilient in the face of all threats to their survival. When I read Kathy's texts I thought how the strength implied in Yokununna's name—the name used by his own family and fellow countrymen—gelled with the descriptions of him given by two of the Aboriginal men McKinnon had arrested in 1934. He was known, they said, as a "cheeky bugger." He wanted "to fight [the] white fellow." Even before the incident at Uluru, he had been involved in several altercations with station owners and, on at least one occasion, shot and wounded. "All the time," he believed that he could "beat [the] white man." Yokununna—Kurkara, Desert Oak No. 1—led his people's resistance to the invasion of their lands.

Perhaps now, almost a century later, the pointlessness of Yoku-nunna's death might be partly redeemed by the larger purpose that his countrymen and women will claim for him. It is not only his skull that will be returned to Country, but the whole truth of his killing as well.

Kapi Mutitjulu (Mutitjulu Waterhole)

POSTSCRIPT

I n March 2021, Kathy Tozer, Sammy Wilson's partner, filmed Sammy speaking about this book at Uluru. She also translated his brief five-minute talk, which was screened at the Adelaide Festival event on the occasion of the book's publication. Here is my transcription of Sammy's words from the video.

> *I'm talking to you about this book that brings a story to light for people so they can reflect and learn from it. It's been hidden for years and years and years. Now it's come out. At some time, we have to speak the truth. Truth-telling. On the record. We made the Uluru Statement for understanding and working together. So, I'm very glad this book has been published for you all to see and you can enjoy being there [in Adelaide] right now to witness this paper. By "paipa" I mean book, it's on paper.*
>
> *The Anangu record of what happened is here [pointing to Uluru behind him]. What happened is right here, in history. We've thought about this story over and over and over, and only now we see what parts were kept secret. My grandfather and others told this story over and over until they passed away.*

They were honest about their story. It should all come out. The things we know that haven't been talked about openly. We are bringing them out. And this is what happened here. It's very important because they left this place because the policeman shot him like that [raising his hands]. They left and didn't come back. When whitefellas arrived afterward they thought this place was "dry"—empty and arid. It's not dry—people lived throughout this land with expert knowledge of it. But the whitefella hunted them away. They left in fear of being shot. So when other people [non-Indigenous] came they did their own thing. "Oh look at this! We can do something here, it's a good magic place." But No. This is a home, Anangu land. So it's a good thing that this book has come out. You can read it, you can talk about it, keep your eye on things. Spread the word, show others, "Hey, take a look at this. Look at it."

Things didn't just happen over that way and that way. The same thing happened right here as well [pointing again to Uluru, behind him]. My grandfather was one of them. This is family we're talking about and they've been hidden away somewhere. And we hope to bring them back; bring him back from the museum where he was hidden away for so long. We have our own museum right here. It's right here in this bushland—home. He should be returned to his home country. He's been lying in a distant museum. Can you imagine that? Shot and taken away to a museum and forgotten like many others. We want the truth to come out. More people need to hear this so more people can understand and let others know. Feel it—imagine it, reflect and feel something. When you read, think about it! [Return to Uluru] tells the story truthfully. Think what else is hidden, something hidden over there and over there. Tell it straight. In Australia we need to think consciously and understand properly and realize certain things. It's up to each and every one of us to recognize: "Oh, OK, this is how things are."

OK. So I'm all the way over here when I should have been there with you. But I'm far away. But I'm sending thanks to you for coming together for this.

NOTE ON KEY SOURCES

The complete reference details for all sources appear on first mention online at https://www.sydney.edu.au/arts/about/our-people/academic -staff/mark-mckenna.html. McKinnon's personal archive includes his original patrol books, correspondence, press clippings, unpublished memoirs, personal documents, photographs, library of books on central Australian history (some annotated), and select artworks. Thanks to the generosity of Susan Golledge and family, this collection is currently in the process of being moved to the Northern Territory Archives. As a result, while much of the material I've drawn on for this book is accessible in public collections and newspaper archives, the sources I've consulted in McKinnon's personal archive will soon become publicly available. In the meantime, it's possible to find numerous examples of McKinnon's recollections. The transcripts of McKinnon's two interviews with the oral history unit at the Northern Territory Archives (with Harry Giese in 1981 and Francis Good in 1991) are available from the NT Archives, together with police records, many of McKinnon's photographs, and some of his unpublished memoirs. The NT Archives also hold the climbing registers that were kept at the top of the rock (1966–86). McKinnon's police staff files are also held at the NT Archives (NTRS 2735 P1).

The National Archives holds the inquest into Kai-Umen's death: "Inquest Kai-Umen (Aboriginal); Held at Alice Springs, 17/1/35," National Archives of Australia, CRS E72/2 Item DL444, and the "Commonwealth Board of Inquiry into Alleged Ill-Treatment of Aboriginals by Constable Bill McKinnon and Others," 1935, National Archives of Australia A1, 1935/1613. The inquiry's report contains most of the relevant correspondence to (and between) the Northern Territory administration and the Commonwealth regarding the shooting at Uluru and McKinnon's treatment of Aboriginal prisoners, including McKinnon's narrative of events, "Story of the Escape of Six Prisoners." For the board's visit to the scene of the killing at Uluru, Charles Mountford's diary and Ted Strehlow's field journals are essential. Mountford's can be downloaded online from the State Library of South Australia, https://collections.slsa.sa.gov.au/resource/PRG+1218/5/3/32; while Strehlow's account can be accessed from the Strehlow Research Centre in Alice Springs or the National Library of Australia. Barry Hill's biography of Strehlow (*Broken Song: T.G.H. Strehlow and Aboriginal Possession*, Milsons Point, NSW: Knopf, 2002) also contains a penetrating account of his time with the board of inquiry in 1935.

By far the most important secondary sources on the shooting are James Warden, "T.G.H. Strehlow and the 1935 Board of Inquiry into the Alleged Ill-Treatment of Aborigines," in *Traditions in the Midst of Change: Communities, Cultures and the Strehlow Legacy in Central Australia: Proceedings of the Strehlow Conference, Alice Springs, 18–20 September 2002*, ed. Michael Cawthorn (Alice Springs, NT: Strehlow Research Centre, 2004), pp. 89–100; Justin O'Brien, "Neither Justified nor Warranted: The 1935 Cleland Inquiry" (draft), available online at https://www.academia.edu/5682141/Neither_justified_nor_warranted_the_1935_Cleland_Inquiry; and Barry Hill, *The Rock:*

Travelling to Uluru (St. Leonards, NSW: Allen & Unwin, 1994). For broader historical context on Aboriginal people in central Australia, Tim Rowse's work is essential: Tim Rowse, "The Centre: A Limited Colonisation," in *Australians from 1939*, eds. Ann Curthoys, A. W. Martin, and Tim Rowse (Broadway, NSW: Fairfax, Syme & Weldon Associates, 1987), pp. 151–66; Tim Rowse, *Indigenous and Other Australians Since 1901* (Sydney: University of New South Wales Press, 2017); Tim Rowse, *White Flour, White Power: From Rations to Citizenship in Central Australia* (Cambridge: Cambridge University Press, 1998). Other essential works include Alan Powell, *Forgotten Country: A Short History of Central Australia* (North Melbourne, VI: Australian Scholarly Publishing, 2018); Ann McGrath, *Born in the Cattle: Aborigines in Cattle Country* (Sydney: Allen & Unwin, 1987); Peter Read and Jay Read, *Long Time, Olden Time: Aboriginal Accounts of Northern Territory History* (Alice Springs, NT: Institute for Aboriginal Development, 1991); Julie Marcus, *The Indomitable Miss Pink: A Life in Anthropology* (Canada Bay, NSW: LhR Press, 2017; first published 2001); and David Carment et al., *Northern Territory Dictionary of Biography* (Darwin: Charles Darwin University Press, 2008).

For Indiginous accounts of the events at Uluru in 1934, David Roberts's 1986 film *Uluru: An Anangu Story* is invaluable, as is David Batty's film of Joseph Donald sitting on the ground at Docker River in the very same year and recounting the story in extraordinary detail, www.youtube.com/watch?v=1TN2IFgIcEI; Jen Cowley's *I Am Uluru: A Family's Story* (Uluru, NT: Uluru Family, 2018) is without peer because it contains a series of Anangu oral histories compiled in close collaboration with the Uluru family. On the challenge posed by the Uluru Statement from the Heart, philosopher Duncan Ivison's *Can Liberal States Accommodate Indigenous Peoples?* (Cambridge: Polity Press, 2020) is essential reading, as is Megan Davis, "The Long Road to Uluru" (www.griffithreview.com/articles/long-road-uluru -walking-together-truth-before-justice-megan-davis/), and every

LIST OF ILLUSTRATIONS

All images from the McKinnon collection are courtesy of Susan Golledge and family.

3   Central Australia (Alan Laver).

6–7   Marree, South Australia, 2013 (Mark McKenna).

13   Inspector Bill McKinnon in the Jubilee Day Parade, Alice Springs, 1951 (National Gallery of Victoria, Melbourne Accessioned, 1984; this digital record has been made available on NGV Collection Online through the generous support of Professor AGL Shaw AO Bequest).

17   McKinnon on Bondi Beach, 1920s (McKinnon collection).

19   McKinnon looking over Alice Springs (Bill McKinnon, McKinnon collection).

21   Alice Springs from Anzac Hill, circa 1935 (Museums Victoria Collections, https://collections.museumsvictoria.com.au/items /771593, accessed July 22, 2020).

22   Kath Rice and Kit Robinson's café, Alice Springs, 1930s (McKinnon collection).

LIST OF ILLUSTRATIONS

LIST OF ILLUSTRATIONS

ACKNOWLEDGMENTS

Return to Uluru grew out of my previous book, *From the Edge: Australia's Lost Histories* (2016), which explored the histories of four places on the littoral edge of the continent that also resided on the edge of Australians' historical consciousness. My shift from the edge to the center took an unexpected turn when I discovered Bill McKinnon's story. Writing this book has reminded me how our best-laid plans for the books we intend to write can often be overturned by what we discover along the way. At some point, McKinnon hijacked my book and I decided not to resist. I slowly came to see that my original plans could be realized even more effectively by writing a history of the center through the story of his life, or more precisely, the biography of one moment in his life. In the next few years, this book will be followed by another, more personal in focus, which will reflect on the histories of places that I've lived in, both in Australia and overseas. The end result, I hope, will be a trilogy of a kind: unbound and misshapen, but true to my research, reading, and thinking over the past decade.

This book could never have been completed without the assistance of friends and the generosity of the families who inherited its histories long before I arrived on the scene. My first thanks go to Edwin Ride. His willingness to share his knowledge of the center (and his camping skills!) made this book possible. Edwin's enthusiasm never wavered, and I've benefited enormously from the many conversations we've had over the years. Susan Golledge and her family were extraordinarily generous, inviting me to their home and assisting me at every turn as I worked my way through Bill McKinnon's personal archive. I owe a particular debt to Susan, Ian, and Matt Golledge, who always recognized the larger purpose of this history. My special thanks go to Matt Golledge. Likewise to Sammy Wilson and Kathy Tozer, who always offered their support and were willing to share their knowledge. I will never forget August 12, 2020, when I met Sammy, Kathy, and Reggie and Cassidy Uluru at Mutitjulu Waterhole. My sincere thanks to all of you.

Anna Russo, Aboriginal heritage and repatriation manager at the South Australian Museum, has walked with me every step of the way since she confirmed that Yokununna's skull resided in the museum's collection of human remains. My thanks also go to Anna's colleague at the museum, John Carty, head of humanities. The trailblazing work of James Warden and Justin O'Brien on the events at Uluru in 1934 and their readiness to offer advice have proved invaluable. Whenever I confronted unexpected U-turns and discoveries, I spoke with James and he helped to keep my eyes on the broader significance of the story. Several people assisted me with research inquiries and contacts: Jen Cowley, whose magnificent book *I Am Uluru: A Family's Story* is surely the definitive history of the Uluru family; filmmaker David Batty, who "got" the story from the first moment; Elisabeth Marnie at the Northern Territory Archives; Neil Bell for his assistance translating key sections of Joseph Donald's testimony; Andrew Sergeant at the National Library of Australia; Mark McAdie; John Dallwitz; Linda Rive; Joy Lai; Joe Potts; and Noel Coulthard.

ACKNOWLEDGMENTS

John Blay, James Boyce, Stephen Fitzpatrick, Tom Griffiths, Marcia Langton, Robert Manne, Mark O'Neill, and Cathy Perkins read the draft manuscript in various stages of its development and made extremely helpful suggestions. My thanks to each of you for traveling with me. Your advice and conversation helped enormously and still does. Many other friends, colleagues, and family have listened patiently as I've regaled them with the latest version of "the story." As ever, I'm indebted to the research and teaching culture in the history department at the University of Sydney. Sincere thanks to all my colleagues and postgraduate and honors students.

My thanks also to Stuart Ward, Bain Attwood, Jan Bruck, Iain McCalman, Sally Heath, Ann Curthoys, John Docker, Peter Hobbins, Ben Armstrong, Moya McKenna, Geraldine McKenna, John Carrick, Michael Joyce, Ockert and Meiri Meyer, Ross Gengos, Peter and Genief Koutsoukis, Catherine McGrath and Martin Dwyer, Martin Harris and Louise Hopson, Ben Wellings and Shanti Sumartojo, Dave Clarke and Jennifer Balint, Rory Slater and Lyn Turner, Edwin and Sharon Ride, Julia Stiles and Michael Walker, Sue O'Rourke, Tim O'Rourke, Robert Morrell, and Christine Freudenstein.

To Lyn Tranter, my literary agent for the last decade and more, thanks for your wise counsel, understanding, and good humor. I'm indebted to Stephen Morrow, my editor at Penguin Random House in New York, who made many helpful suggestions and has contributed enormously to shaping the book for US readers. My thanks also go to Stephen's editorial assistant, Grace Layer. To my Australian publishers at Black Inc., Morry Schwartz and Chris Feik, and my editor, Kirstie Innes-Will, thanks for your support, intellectual engagement, and unfailing commitment to making this book "the best version of itself."

To my siblings and their partners: Chris McKenna and Deborah Hoffman, Adrian McKenna and Kristen Daglish-Rose, Kieran and

INDEX

Note: Italicized page numbers indicate material in photographs or illustrations.

ABOUT THE AUTHOR

Mark McKenna is one of Australia's leading historians, based at the University of Sydney. He is the author of several prizewinning books, including *From the Edge: Australia's Lost Histories*, *Looking for Black-fellas' Point*, and *An Eye for Eternity: The Life of Manning Clark*, which won the Prime Minister's Literary Award for nonfiction.